PINK

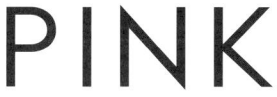

Hayley Edwards-Dujardin

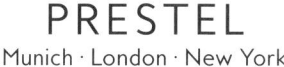

PRESTEL

Munich · London · New York

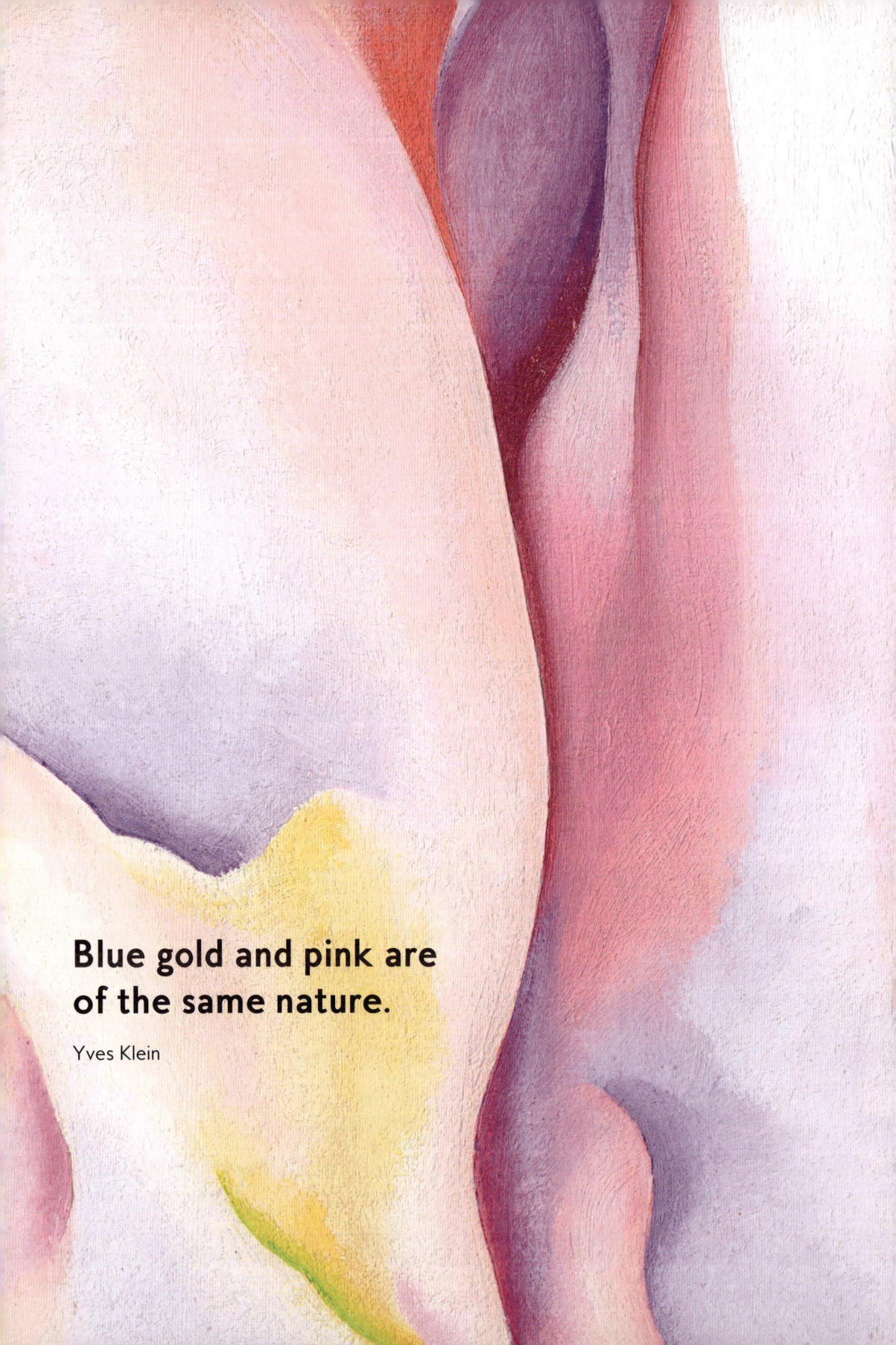

**Blue gold and pink are
of the same nature.**

Yves Klein

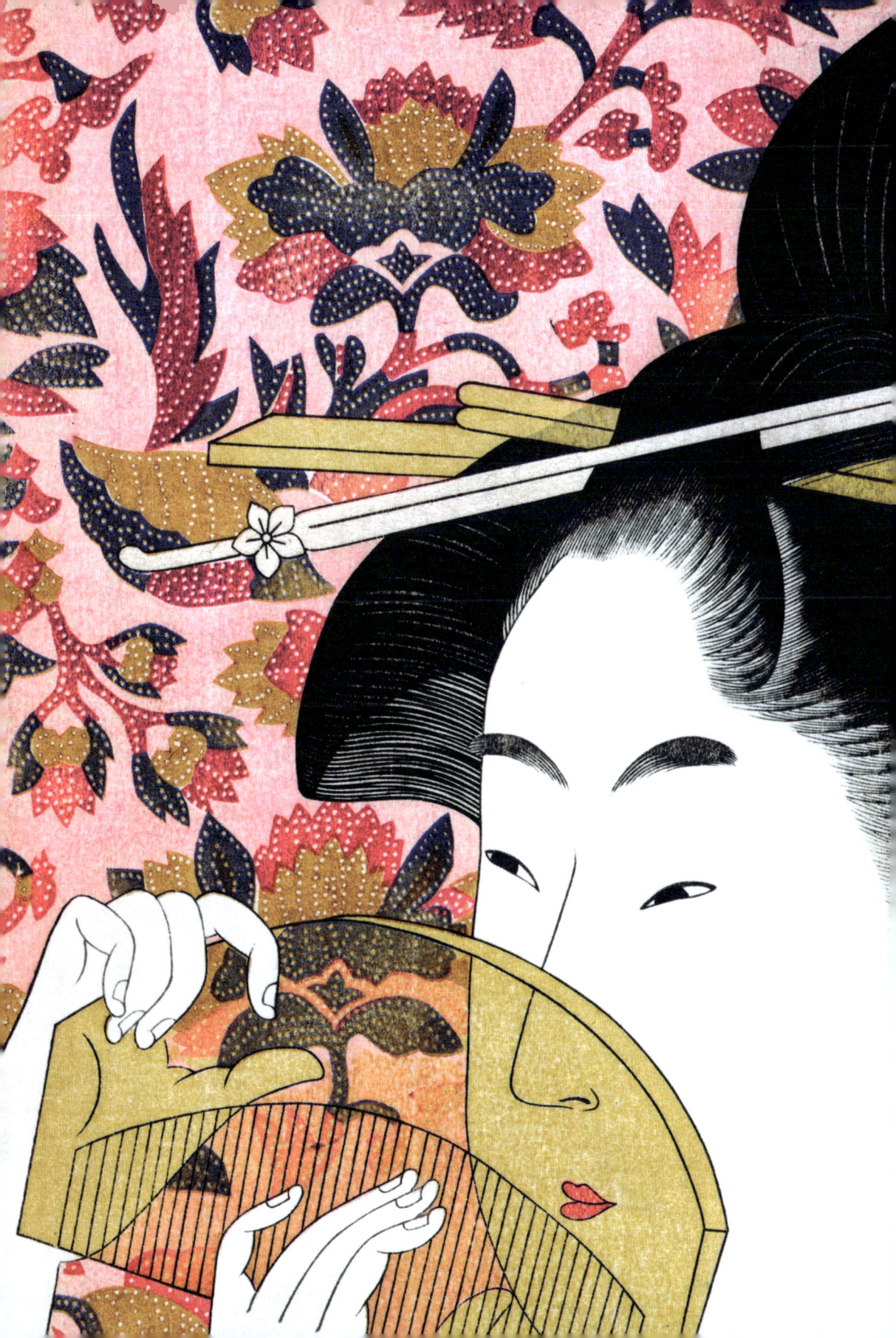

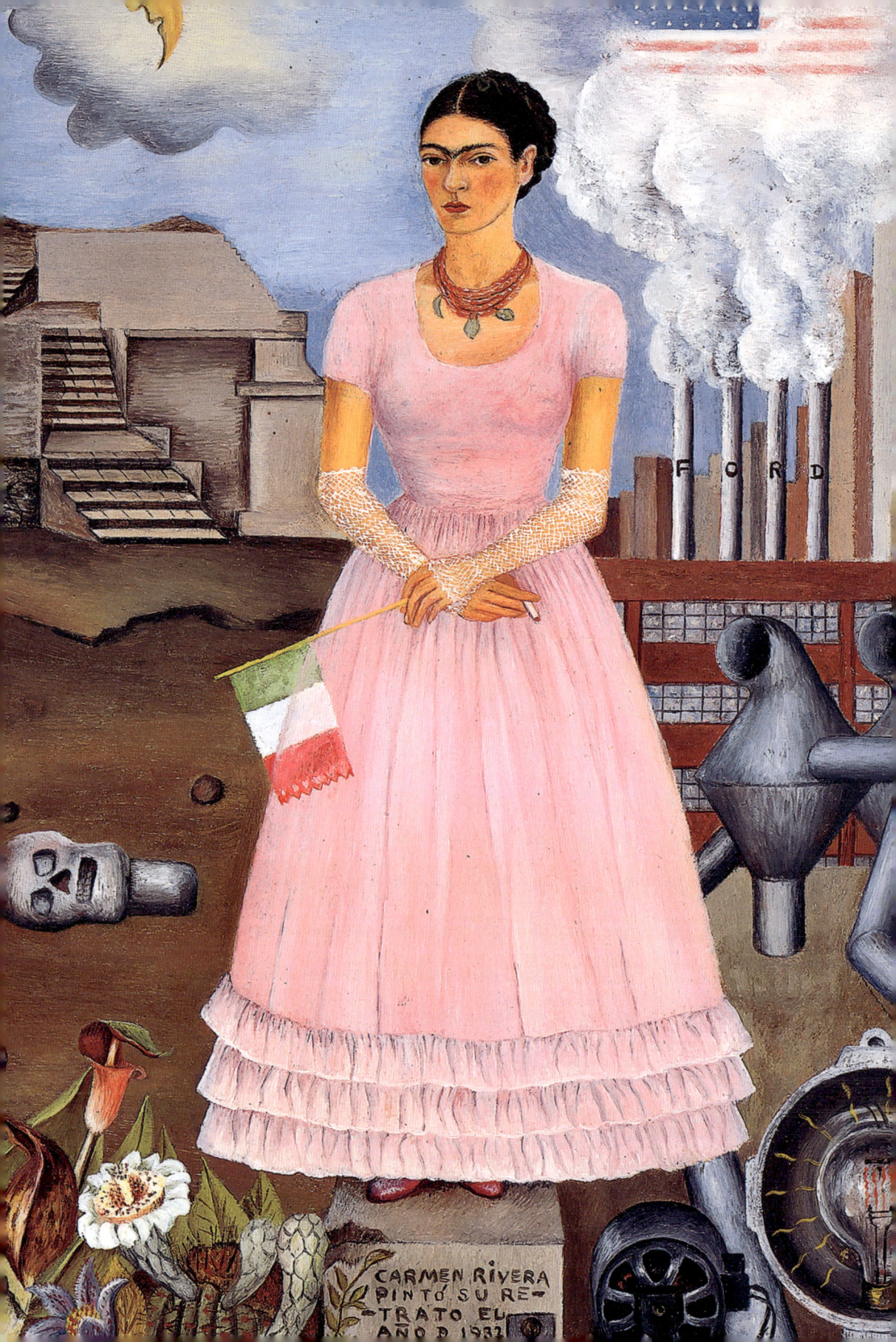

FORD

CARMEN RIVERA
PINTÓ SU RE-
-TRATO EL
AÑO D 1932

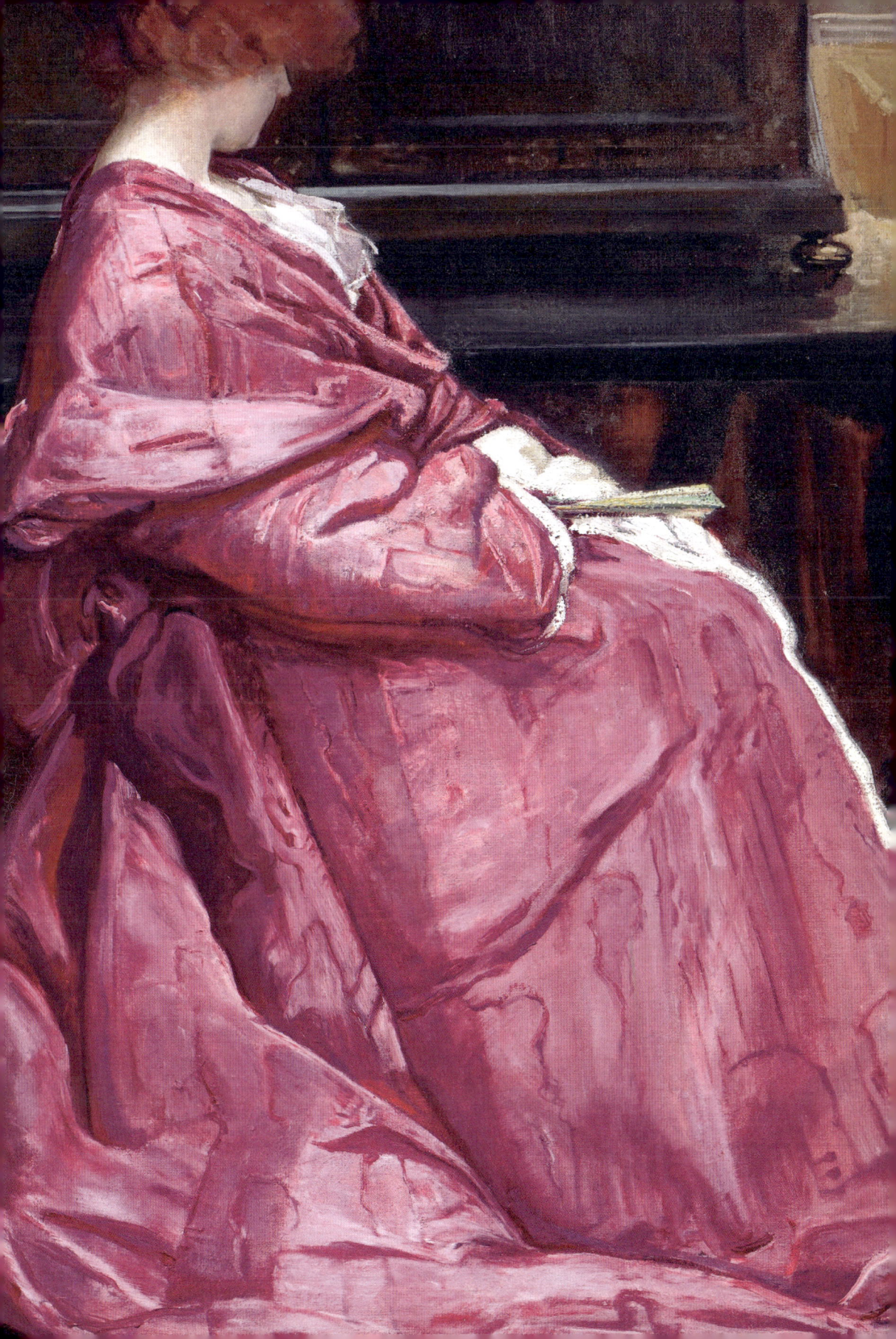

Pink in Art

What do we know about pink? Firstly, there are all the stereotypes with which we have been confronted since childhood: pink the prerogative of little girls, pink the colour of tenderness and love . . . Yet pink's many variations play on its ambivalences and contradictions.

Puce

Marie-Antoinette's entourage were fond of inventing colourful expressions to describe the tints of her extravagant wardrobe. For one dress, midway between grey, brown and pink, the term couleur de puce ('flea colour') was coined. This gave rise to a series of variations: cuisse de puce (flea's thigh), ventre de puce (flea's belly), dos de puce (flea's back) . . .

To Each a Colour

In the twentieth century, blue was assigned to boys and pink to girls. By the beginning of the Second World War, baby clothes obeyed this distinction and with the growth of consumer society and its excesses dolls and princesses were dressed in pink. Pop Art understood this, Conceptual Art denounced it.

Naming Pink

According to science, pink does not exist in nature. As a pigment, it is a mixture of two supreme colours, red and white. So, since the dawn of time, pink has been regarded as inferior, subordinate to the all-powerful red of which it is merely a pale shade. Yet this did not prevent authors in antiquity from describing it, because pink expresses sensations and feelings. And perhaps because it is so enigmatic, pink has been given a host of names: crimson when it is the colour of flesh, dawn pink when it tints the sky at sunrise, fuchsia when it is the flower of the same name. Pink has been dominated by other colours incapable of letting it express itself on its own, so it is described as orange, coral, violet, beige, etc. Pink becomes the name of everything one wants to explain without really being able to find the right words.

A Pink of Many Colours

In the Middle Ages and during the Renaissance pink was regarded as merely a pale shade of red. Yet it was by no means insignificant because it appears in all its dazzling nuances in majestic portraits representing the privilege of the wealthiest. It can be virile as the cousin of red, bedeck the flowers so essential in religious iconography, and of course it can be the subtle tints of skin. Materialist, spiritual, carnal? Nothing but discordances. And then, with the advent of the Rococo style in the eighteenth century, pink finally got its own back. With their newfound taste for pastel tints, European aristocrats could delight in frivolous scenes in which pink-cheeked protagonists engage in amorous conversations and erotic games.

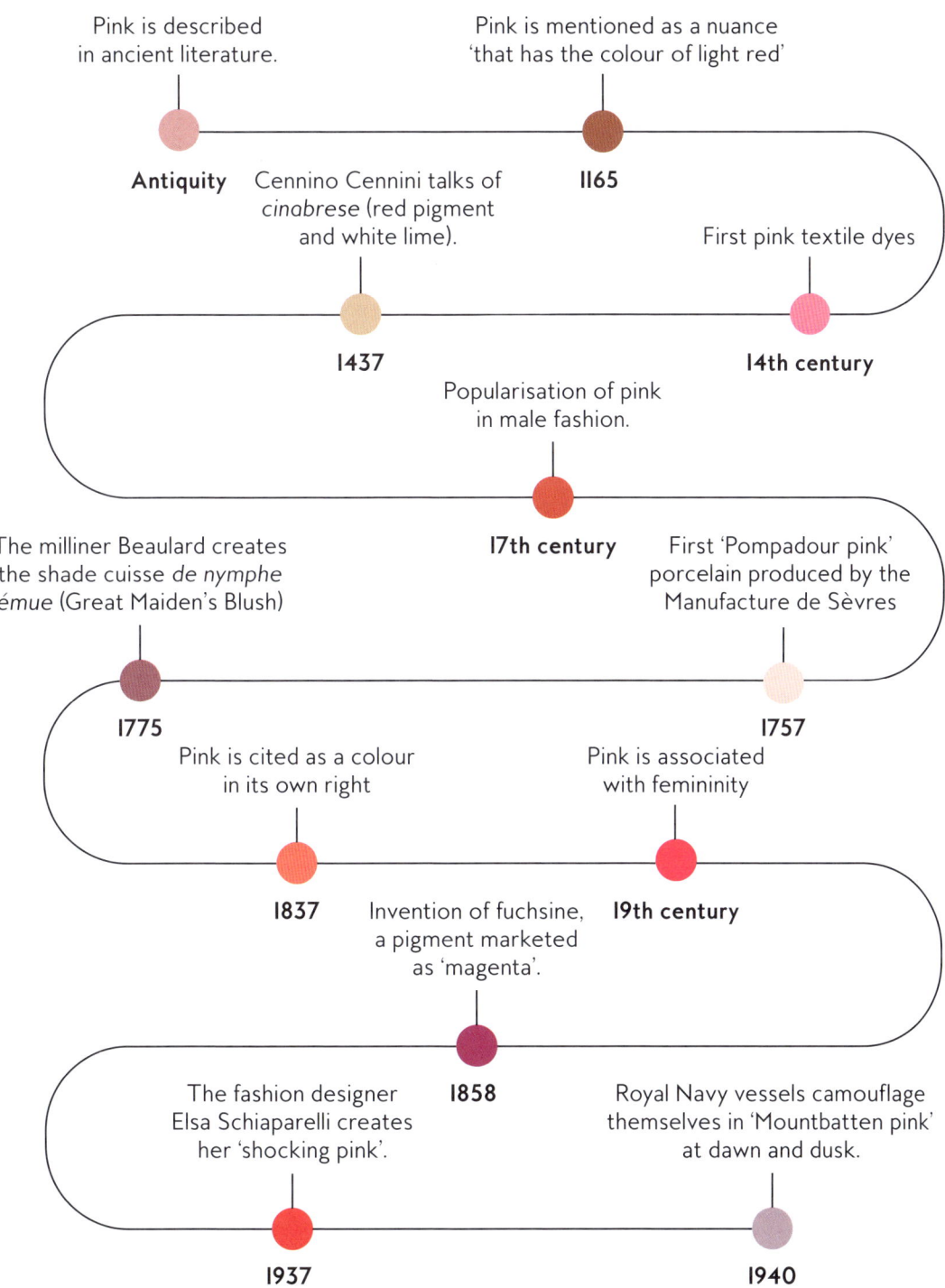

Pink is described in ancient literature.

Pink is mentioned as a nuance 'that has the colour of light red'

Antiquity

Cennino Cennini talks of *cinabrese* (red pigment and white lime).

1165

First pink textile dyes

1437

Popularisation of pink in male fashion.

14th century

The milliner Beaulard creates the shade cuisse *de nymphe émue* (Great Maiden's Blush)

17th century

First 'Pompadour pink' porcelain produced by the Manufacture de Sèvres

1775

Pink is cited as a colour in its own right

Pink is associated with femininity

1757

1837

Invention of fuchsine, a pigment marketed as 'magenta'.

19th century

The fashion designer Elsa Schiaparelli creates her 'shocking pink'.

1858

Royal Navy vessels camouflage themselves in 'Mountbatten pink' at dawn and dusk.

1937

1940

A white rose in truth she might be, that a butterfly has made blush, when full of ardour, it made free, and, against her, chose to brush.

Théophile Gautier, 'La Rose-thé', 1852

Sensual Pink

In 1920, Marcel Duchamp created a fictive female double, Rrose Sélavy ('Eros c'est la vie' when said), to whom he attributed her own literary and artistic production. In 1922, the poet Robert Desnos also made use of Rrose Sélavy as the imaginary author of several of his aphorisms.

Revenge Wears Pink

In 2016 Anish Kapoor controversially acquired the rights for Vantablack, an ultra-matte black pigment and retained exclusive use of it. Thumbing his nose at this, the artist Stuart Semple imagined a pink pigment, 'the world's pinkest pink', and sold it to everyone except Anish Kapoor.

Revolution or Regression?

Should one really believe that it was in the era of Rococo frivolity that pink became a feminine colour? Certainly not, because there are many portraits of men dressed in pink. Yes, Rococo can be regarded as a frivolous style, but this frivolity was enjoyed not solely by those unconcerned by material contingencies. To wear pink was an assertion of power, a sign of the arrogance of a society dissociated from the real world.

Everything changed after the French Revolution. Gone the insignia of aristocracy, gone all its frills and furbelows. Colour was abandoned for black, a black in which to better distinguish oneself. Distinguish oneself from whom? From women, of course, from those inferior creatures for whom the game of appearances is the sole amusement tolerated by a misogynistic society.

But with time, things could only get better. During the Industrial Revolution the invention of chemical pigments increased the nuances available to artists and couturiers. Women could now bedeck themselves in pink and painters could again depict them as sensual, domesticated, infantile creatures. The gradual feminisation of pink was underway. Pink could be used to mock, stigmatise, incense, embellish or charm. Pink now had a life of its own.

Rosa Mollissimo,
Pierre-Joseph Redouté
1817–24
Lithograph
Private collection

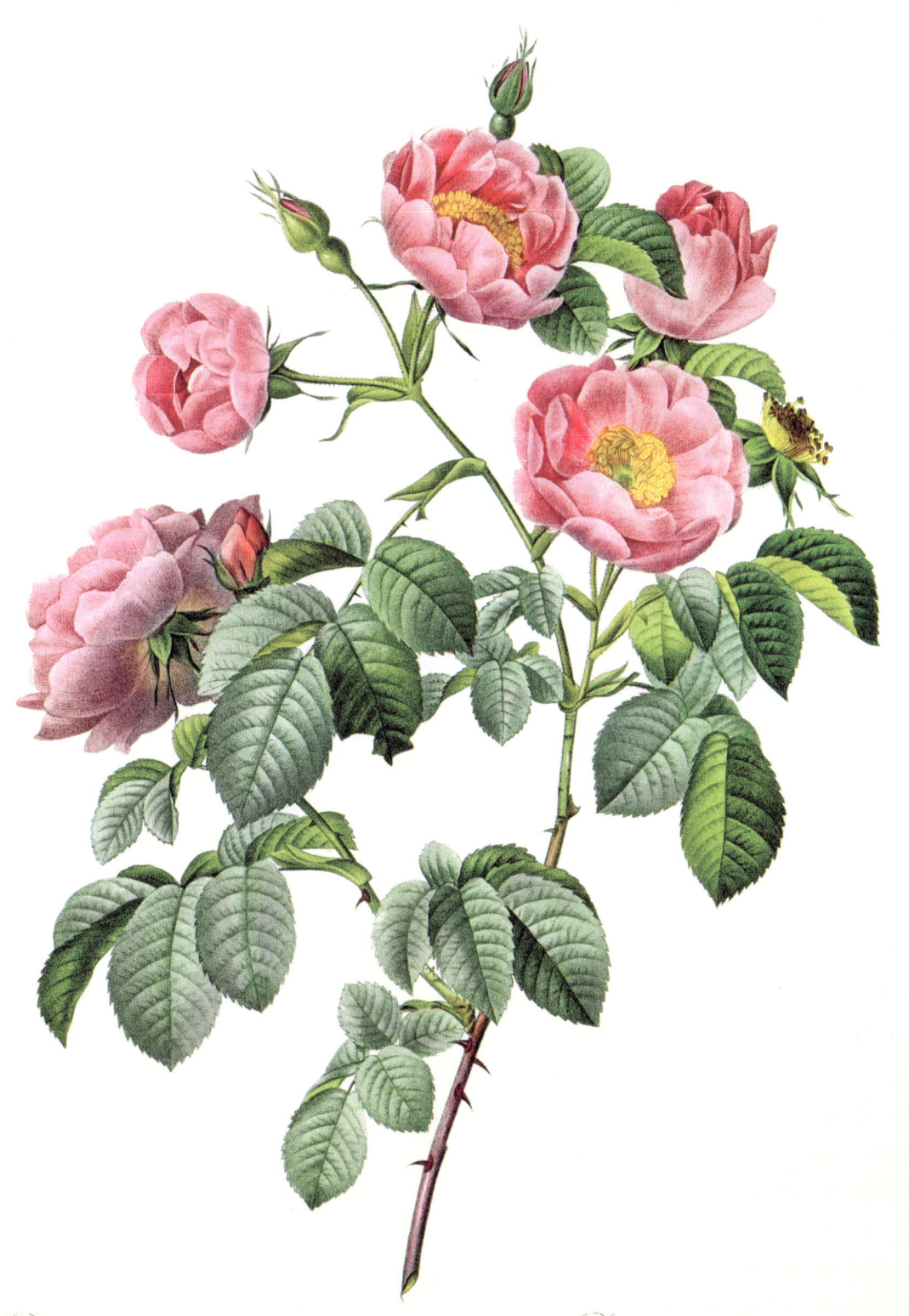

Rosa mollissima.

Rosier à feuilles molles.

P. J. Redouté pinx.

Imprimerie de Remond

Victor sculp.

The Geography of Pink

The Geography of Pink

Lakes and Rivers

Lake Retba
Senegal

Lake Hillier
Australia

Rivière la Rose
Guadeloupe

Beaches and shorelines

Spiaggia rosa
Maddalena archipelago,
Italy

Pink Sands Beach
Harbour Island,
Bahamas

Salinas de Galerazamba
Colombia

Mountains and valleys

Monte Rosa
Swiss Alps

Rose Valley
Bulgaria

Valley of the Roses
Morocco

Towns and cities

Toulouse
France

Jaipur
India

Petra
Jordan

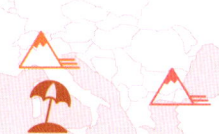

The Compass Rose

Phoenician seafarers
were the first to use the
compass rose in navigation.
It indicates the four
cardinal points and the
intermediate directions,
originally eight, now as
many as thirty-two.

Pink Skies

As the sun sets or rises
it traverses a greater
thickness of atmosphere.
Azote and oxygen
molecules selectively
absorb and scatter the
colour blue and only rays
in the red portion of the
spectrum reach
our eyes.

Chromatic Range

Naming Pink

Pink is a red infused with white whose chromatic range extends from orange to purple and even beige hues. These variations have names such as powder pink, fuchsia, salmon, etc.

Pink was obviously named after the most common colour of the rose flower. In 1905, the Société Française des chrysanthémistes published its own colour chart to aid in determining the colours of flowers, foliage and fruit. Here are some of the nuances it lists and describes.

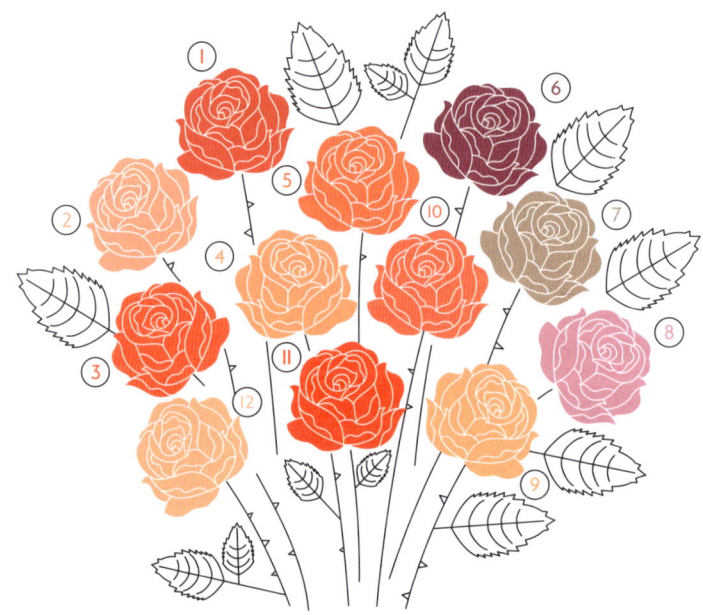

1. **Carthamin pink**
Intermediary colour between salmon and red
2. **Nymph pink**
An allusion to what might be the colour of a nymph's skin
3. **Purple pink**
Pink mixed with Tyrian purple or a shade of carmine purple

4. **Hermosa pink**
Colour of the rose variety unlit by the sun
5. **Salmon pink**
Pink nuanced with a little Cadmium yellow
6 **Vinous pink**
A wine coloured shade of pink

7. **Rose gold**
A pinkish gold used in gilding, rare in the plant world
8. **Lilac pink**
Lilac tinted pink, the colour of the flowers of the Judas tree
9. **Tender pink**
Evoking a light shade of rose madder lake

10. **Bright pink**
A luminous pink evoking a light shade of geranium red
11. **Burnt pink**
Alluding to a light shade of burnt carmine
12. **Flesh pink**
A pink close to skin tint

Flesh

During the Renaissance artists began using this tint to paint faces and hands, usually mixing a red earth pigment and lime.

> Sandro Botticelli (p. 19)
> François Boucher (p. 27)
> Guido Reni (p. 79)

Powder

Certainly the pinkest pink. Gentle and pastel coloured, it has been associated with little girls since the mid-twentieth century. It is referred to as 'rose pink' in books on pigments in the nineteenth century.

> Marie Laurencin (p. 93)
> Frida Kahlo (p. 99)
> Louise Bourgeois (p. 57)

Nymph's Thigh

A pink skin tint invented by a milliner in 1775 reflecting the contemporary fondness for giving romantic names to the colours worn by elegant aristocratic women.

> Edgar Degas (p. 35)
> Jean-Honoré Fragonard (p. 33)

Carmine

In the late seventeenth century, dyers produced a crimson from madder and cochineal. Carmine is a flesh tint resembling the colour of the skin when blushing.

> François Clouet (p. 73)
> Giovanni Battista Moroni (p. 75)

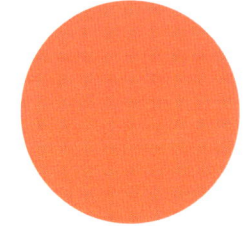

Salmon

The fashion industry was the first to describe a pale, orange-tinted pink as 'salmon' in the 1820s. It owes its name to the colour of salmon roe.

> Pablo Picasso (p. 47)
> James Tissot (p. 39)
> Bronzino (p. 69)

Parma

The term 'Parma' first appeared in the late 1820s, describing a pinkish tint of mauve. It was named after the Parma violets perfume then fashionable.

> Joseph-Siffred Duplessis (p. 83)
> Carlo Crivelli (p. 65)
> Utamaro (p. 31)

Old Rose

The term 'old rose' first appeared in publications on fashion and decoration in the late nineteenth century. It denotes a greyish, slightly mauve pink and also evokes the colour of faded rosewood.

> Guido Reni (p. 79)
> Joseph-Siffred Duplessis (p. 83)

Candy

The expression 'candy pink' established itself in the late nineteenth century. Candy and pink had previously been associated by the Goncourt brothers to somewhat pejoratively describe a sweet, gourmand shade of pink

> Bunel (p. 23)
> Pontormo (p. 67)
> Raoul Dufy (p. 51)

Fuchsia

The fuchsia plant was discovered on the island of Saint-Domingue and fuchsine was invented in 1856 to imitate its colour. For a long time it was predominantly known as fuchsia red.

> Georgia O'Keeffe (p. 95)
> John Humphreys Johnston (p. 85)
> Christo and Jeanne-Claude (p. 55)

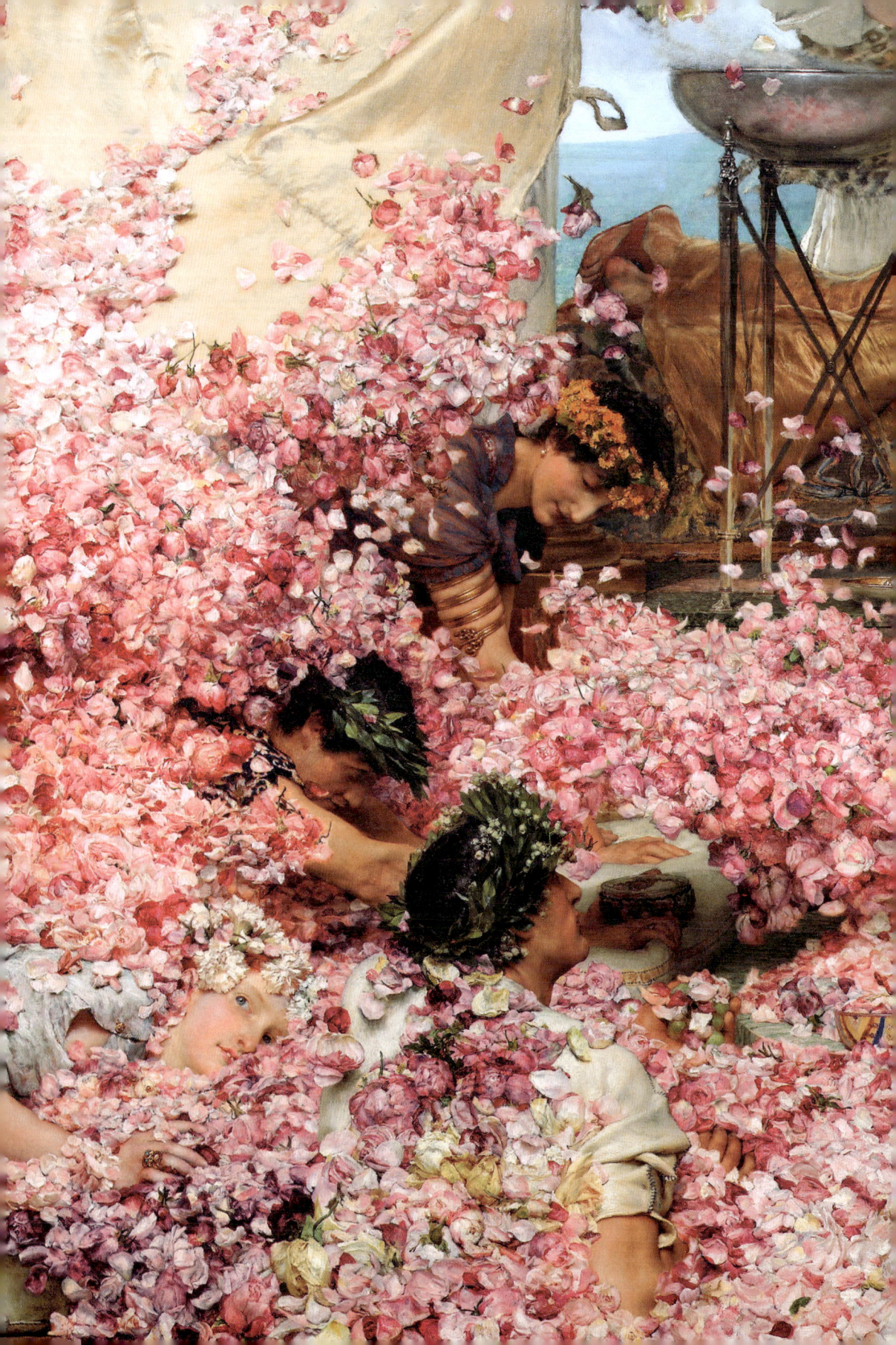

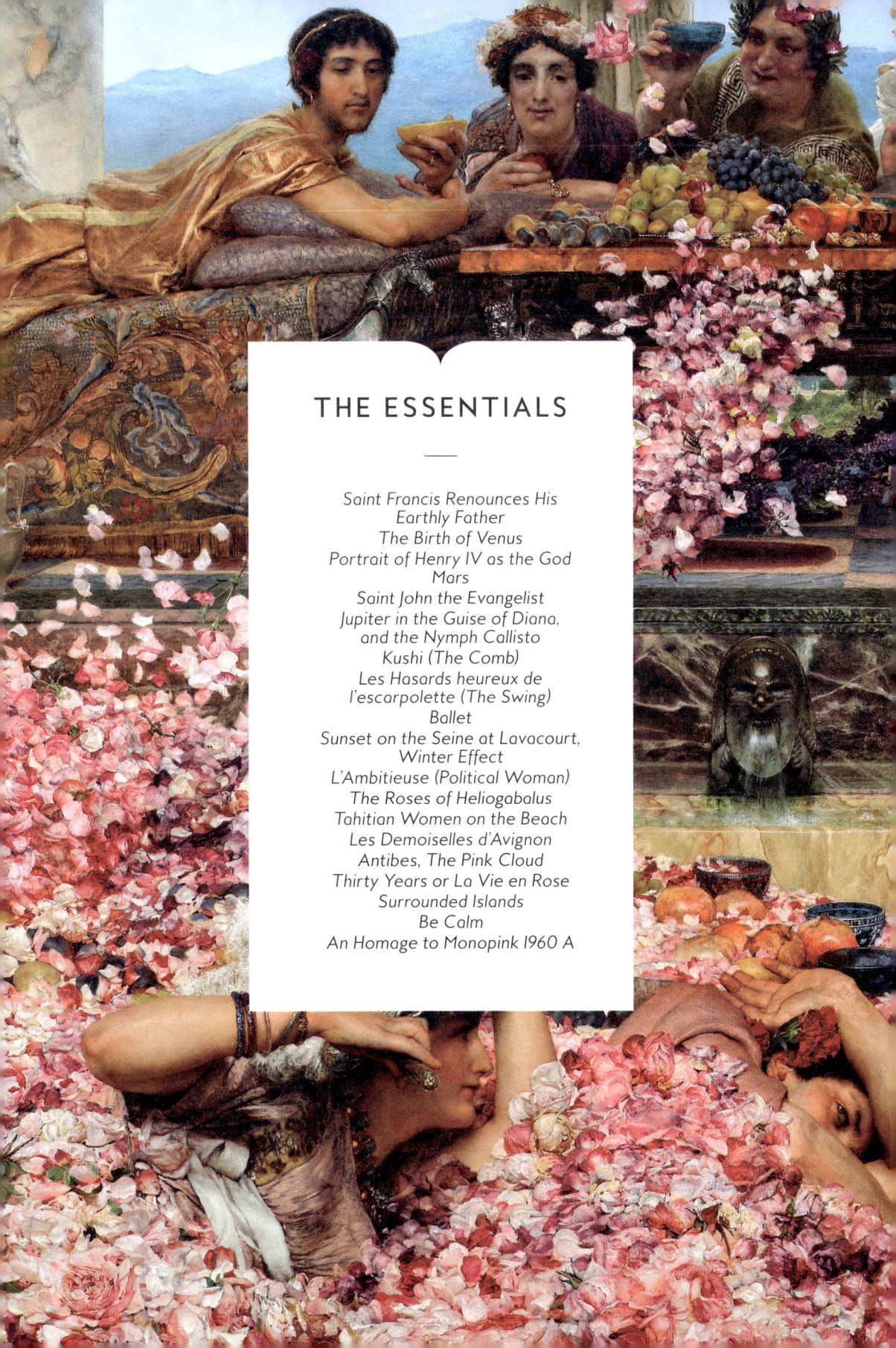

THE ESSENTIALS

—

Saint Francis Renounces His Earthly Father

1437–44

The Other Scenes . . .

The other panels of the *San Sepolcro Altarpiece* are: *Triumph Over Insubordination, Lust and Greed*; *Francis and the Poor Knight* and *Francis's Vision*; *The Marriage of Saint Francis to Lady Poverty*; *Saint Francis Before the Sultan*; *The Wolf of Gubbio*; *The Stigmatisation of Saint Francis*; *The Funeral of Saint Francis*; *Saint Francis Before the Pope: The Granting of the Indulgence of the Portiuncula.*

Between Two Worlds

Having endured the ravages of the Black Death in 1348, in the 1420s the city of Siena again became a major artistic centre with a second generation of artists, one of whom was Sassetta.

In 1437 he received an exceptional commission for the Franciscan church of Borgo San Sepolcro, dedicated to Saint Francis. His task was to paint an altarpiece representing a Madonna on one side and on the other scenes from the saint's life. The altarpiece is regarded as the greatest, most monumental masterpiece of fifteenth-century Sienese art. *Saint Francis Renounces His Earthly Father* is one of its panels.

In this episode in his adoption of an ascetic life, he is shown naked next to the Archbishop of Assisi, who is covering him with an embroidered mantle. The clothes he has taken off are at the feet of his father, who is being held back as he tries to dissuade his son from his foolish idea. Sassetta accentuated the composition's verticality with the pillars and the slender figures, as if to emphasise the spiritual elevation of the future saint. He was also separating the earthly and heavenly worlds with the pink edifice protecting the saint and members of the clergy, which his father is being prevented from entering.

In the Catholic religion, pink symbolises joy and the promise of the coming of light after the night. By plunging us in the pink of the edifice and the figures' garments, we can imagine that Sassetta was inviting us to understand the faith of a man not renouncing the material world but reaching for light.

Saint Francis Renounces His Earthly Father,
Sassetta
1437–44
Tempera on wood
National Gallery, London

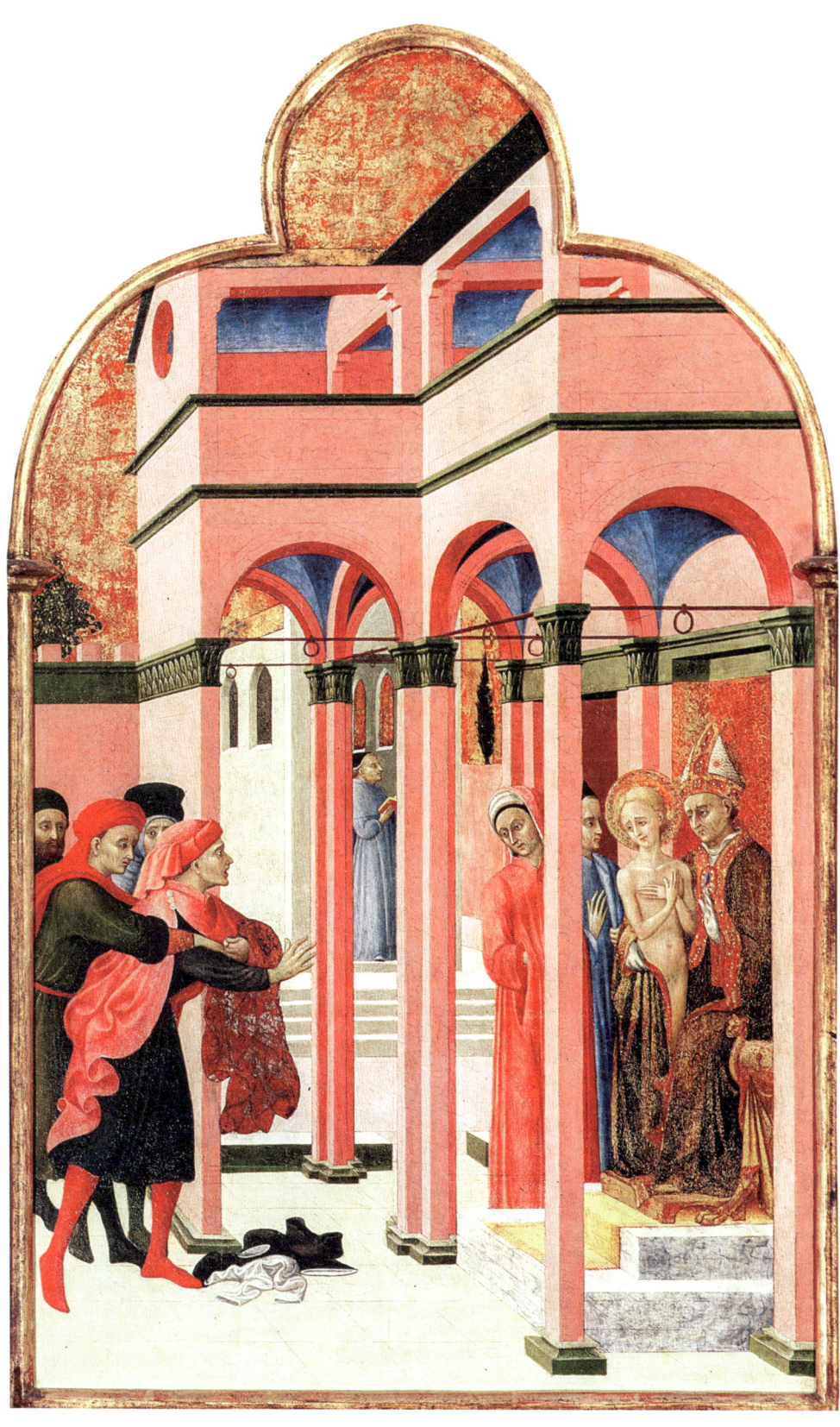

The Birth of Venus

1483–85

The Story of a Birth

'Out of her mother's depths, still cold and steaming, thrown up with bitter heavings into the sun, look, on the belaboured sill of storms, at flesh delivering itself from the diamonds of torment.' Paul Valéry à propos *The Birth of Venus*.

TIMELINE

Happy events

1732	Noël-Nicolas Coypel, *The Birth of Venus*
1848	Jean-Auguste-Dominique Ingres, *Vénus Anadyomene*
1863	Alexandre Cabanel, *The Birth of Venus*
1912	Odilon Redon, *The Birth of Venus*
1984	Andy Warhol, *Details of Renaissance Paintings*
2009	David LaChapelle, *Rebirth of Venus*

A Vision of Beauty

A protégé of the Medicis and motivated by humanist ideas, Sandro Botticelli painted idealist works questioning reality but above all an ideal of beauty, as shown here by Venus emerging from the waves.

Two elements suggest that it was probably a member of the Medici family who commissioned this picture: the presence of orange trees, the dynasty's emblem, and the woman who modelled for the goddess, Simonetta Vespucci, Giuliano de' Medici's mistress.

Although described as the birth of Venus, the picture depicts the goddess reaching the shores of Cyprus, gently borne there by a large scallop pushed by Zephyr, god of the winds, and a nymph. On terra firma, an allegory of spring is awaiting the goddess, readying herself to drape her in a pink, floral-patterned mantle contrasting with her own exquisitely patterned dress. This theme, popularised by Homer, Ovid and the poet Agnolo Poliziano, combined contemporary aesthetics and antique influences.

Botticelli was mixing mirage and nature in an idealised humanist vision. The sea seems to be decorated with scales, myrtle flowers are floating in the air and the graceful, sculpturally depicted figures have pink complexions.

Venus is one of the few goddesses to be portrayed nude in antiquity. She is shown here as a chaste deity with her long hair concealing her pubis and a hand covering one breast. Botticelli is reminding us that this both sensual and modest goddess is embodying beauty, charm, love and fertility in an elegant depiction intended to awaken the senses.

No, the daughter of the seas shall not fear my states.
In my empire Venus was born.

Aeneid, Book V

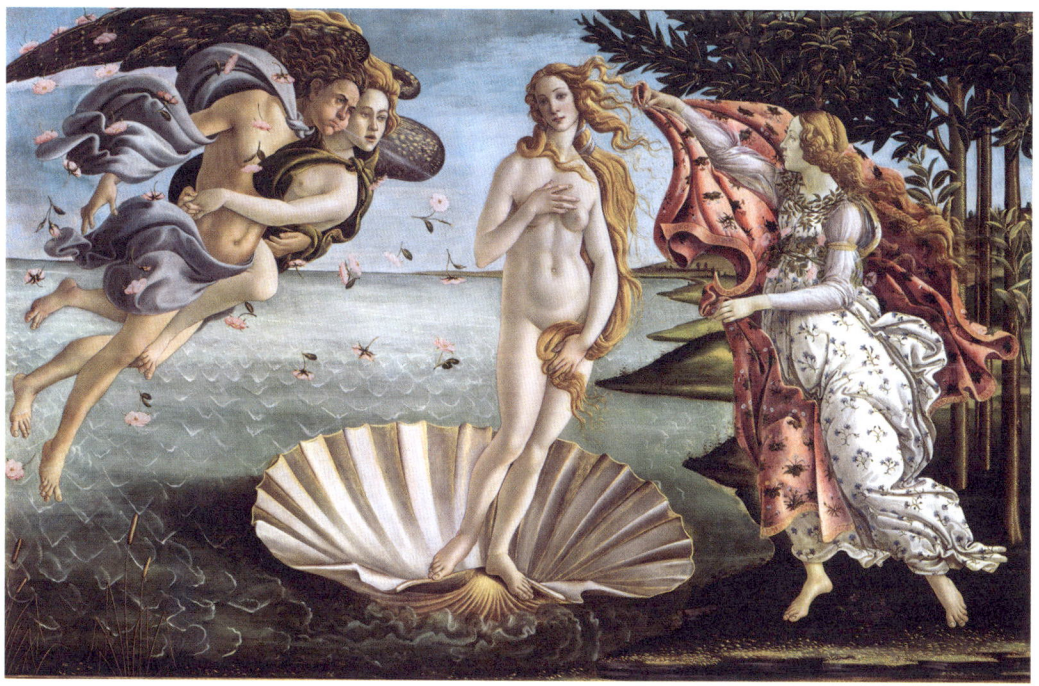

The Birth of Venus,
Sandro Botticelli
1483–85
Tempera on linen canvas
Galerie degli Uffizi, Florence

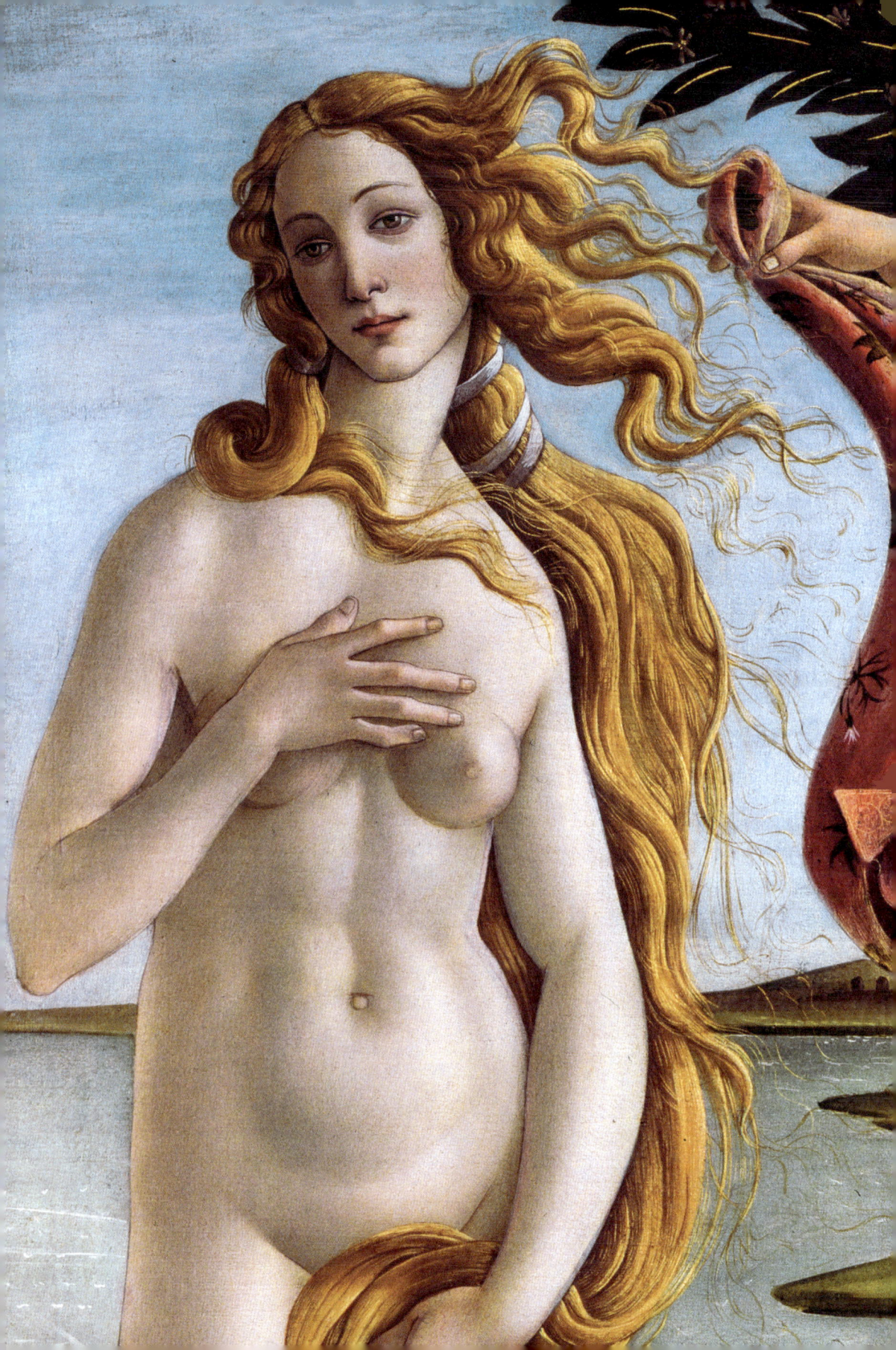

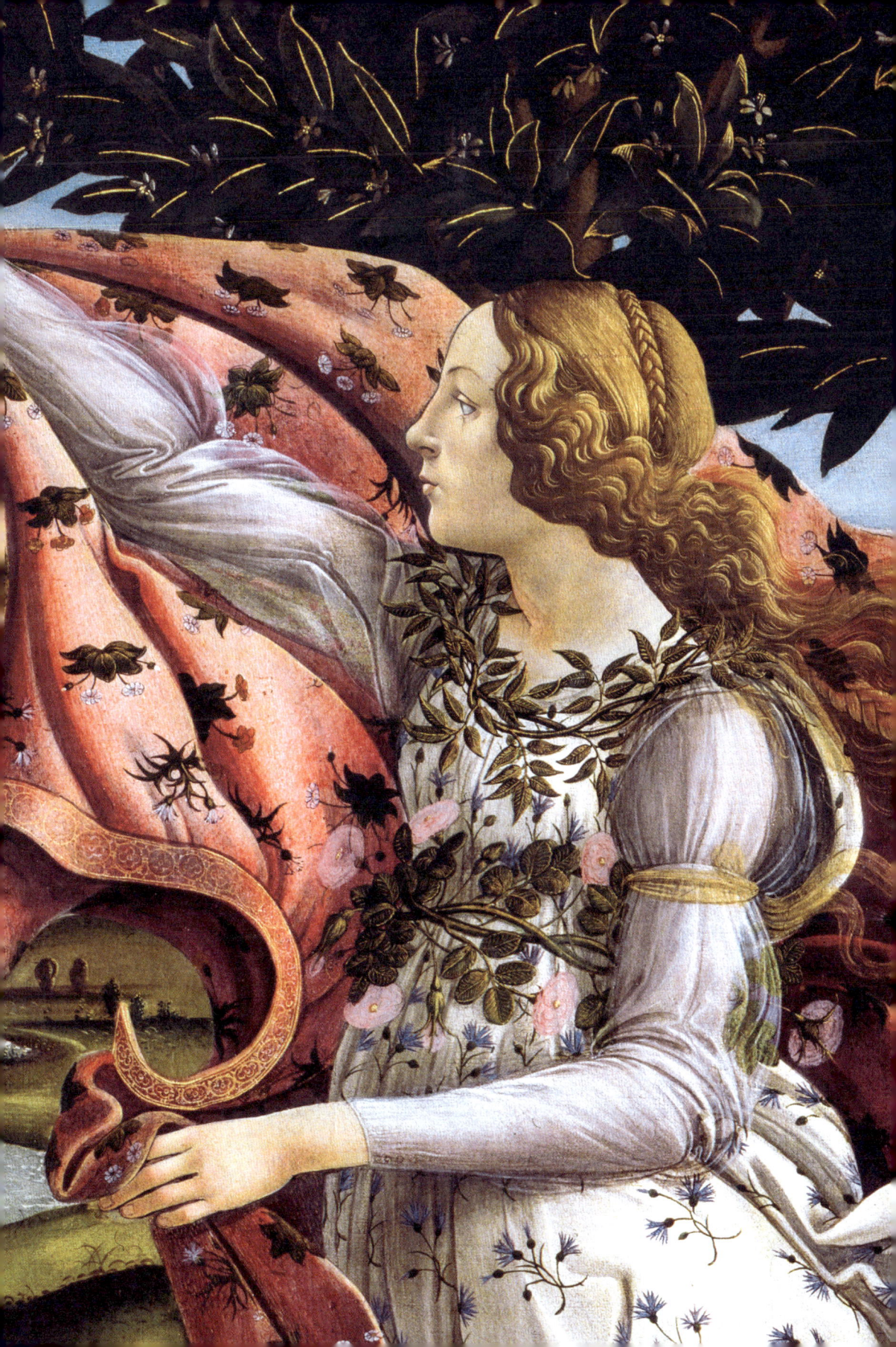

Portrait of Henry IV as the God Mars

1605/6

The War of the Rose

When brazilwood arrived in Europe during the Renaissance, textiles could at last be dyed pink. The colour became popular with the aristocracy, particularly for men.

Today pink has many stereotypes attached to it, notably its supposed female specificity, but it was often associated with masculinity from the Renaissance to the eighteenth century, when Madame de Pompadour popularised it amongst women at court. Pink was then perceived as a shade of red and like red symbolised power and therefore virility.

So it is hardly surprising that Jacob Bunel chose to portray Henri IV in vivid pink armour. This is a triumphant, martial, conquering king appropriating imperial attributes. With his head crowned with laurels he is trampling on his enemies' armour and assertively brandishing his commander's baton. From Mars, god of war, he has borrowed his conquering authority, but instead of red he prefers this vivid pink giving him a certain panache, for the purpose of this portrayal is to temper his warriorlike image. Henri IV is being shown here as a triumphant but also just and benevolent monarch.
Note his gentle smile and kindly eyes. This is a pacific, jovial king.

The pink modifies the gory intensity of red. This is the political, diplomatic, almost propagandist pink of a monarch intent on showing his strength but also his respect for his fellow men.

In the Service of the King

Henri IV was one of the first French kings to realise the importance of portraiture in establishing his political image. This iconographic ambition certainly explains why he is regarded as one of the most popular kings in Franch history.

From Red to Pink

The bark and thick branches of the Pernambuco or brazilwood tree are reduced to shavings then immersed in baths of alkaline water for several hours. It is the effect of the alkali that pinkens the red wood.

Portrait of Henry IV as the God Mars,
Jacob Bunel
1605/6
Oil on canvas
Musée national et domaine du château de Pau

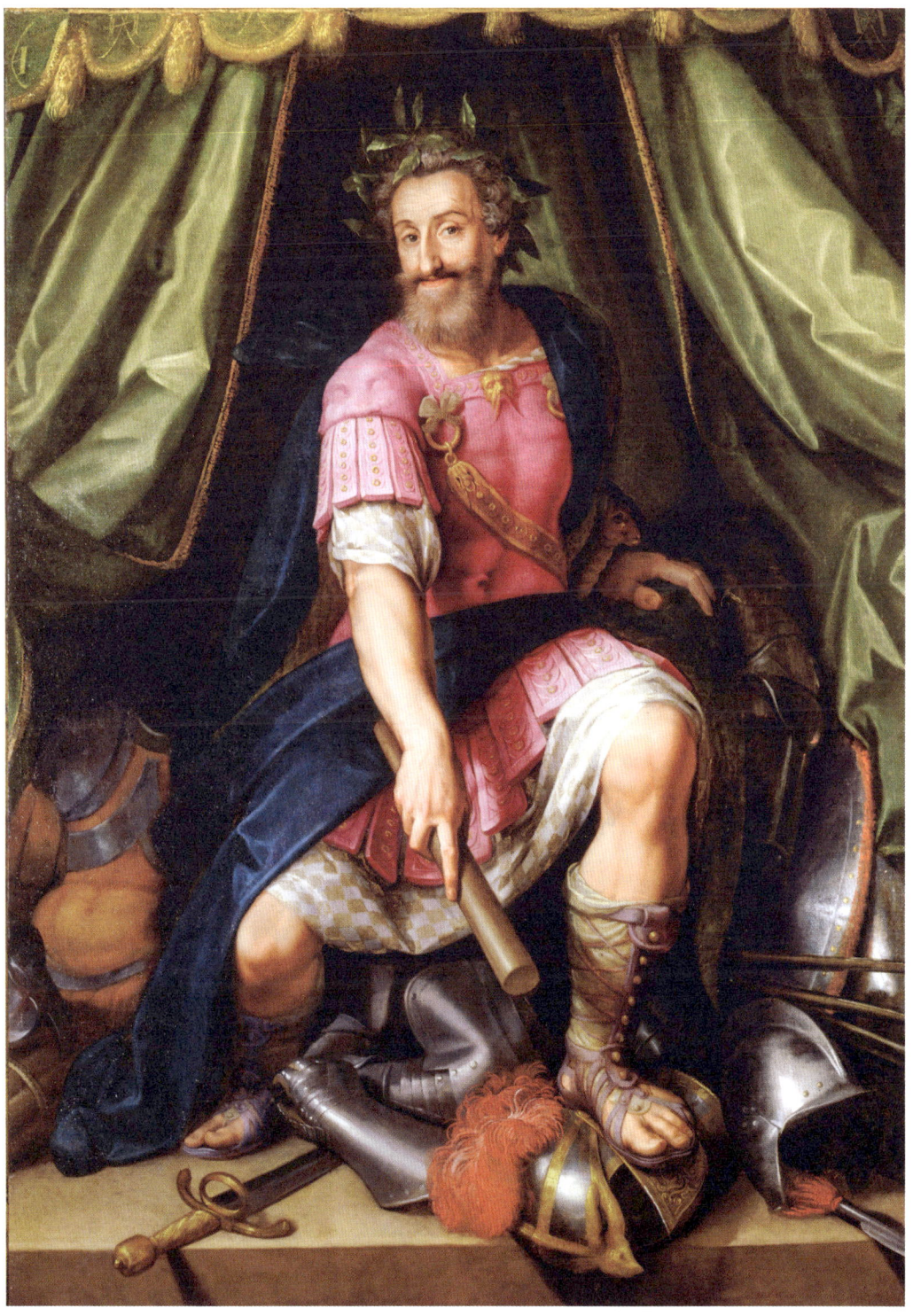

Saint John the Evangelist

1610–14

In His Hands

El Greco's artistic testament, the *Apostolado*, in the Museo de El Greco in Toledo, is one of the rare series on the subject (there are two others, unfinished). It comprises twelve portraits of the apostles and one of Christ.

The series, originally hanging in the poorhouse in Saint-Sebastien, depicts Christ gazing at his entourage, six apostles looking to their right and six to their left. One has to imagine them with their gazes converging on the central Christ. Even if the series appears to be finished, one can clearly see that only three portraits (Christ, Saint Peter and Saint Paul) were definitely completed and that the others are in a more sketch-like state.

This does not prevent this androgynously featured Saint John from embodying a finesse only heightened by El Greco's bold, expressive drawing. With surprising freedom he is reminding us of an episode in the *Golden Legend*, in which the saint, invited to drink poisoned wine from a golden chalice, is spared only when the poison escapes in the form of a snake.

The fervent colours and the green and pink of his tunic seem to both oppose and complement one another with mesmerising vibrancy. His thin, graceful hands seem to be glowing with fiery, almost dancing nuances oscillating between spirituality and materiality. They depict living flesh but are also celestial, ethereal extensions of his divinely radiant garments. Saint John was the first of Christ's disciples, the fieriest and humblest, a duality embodied in this portrait.

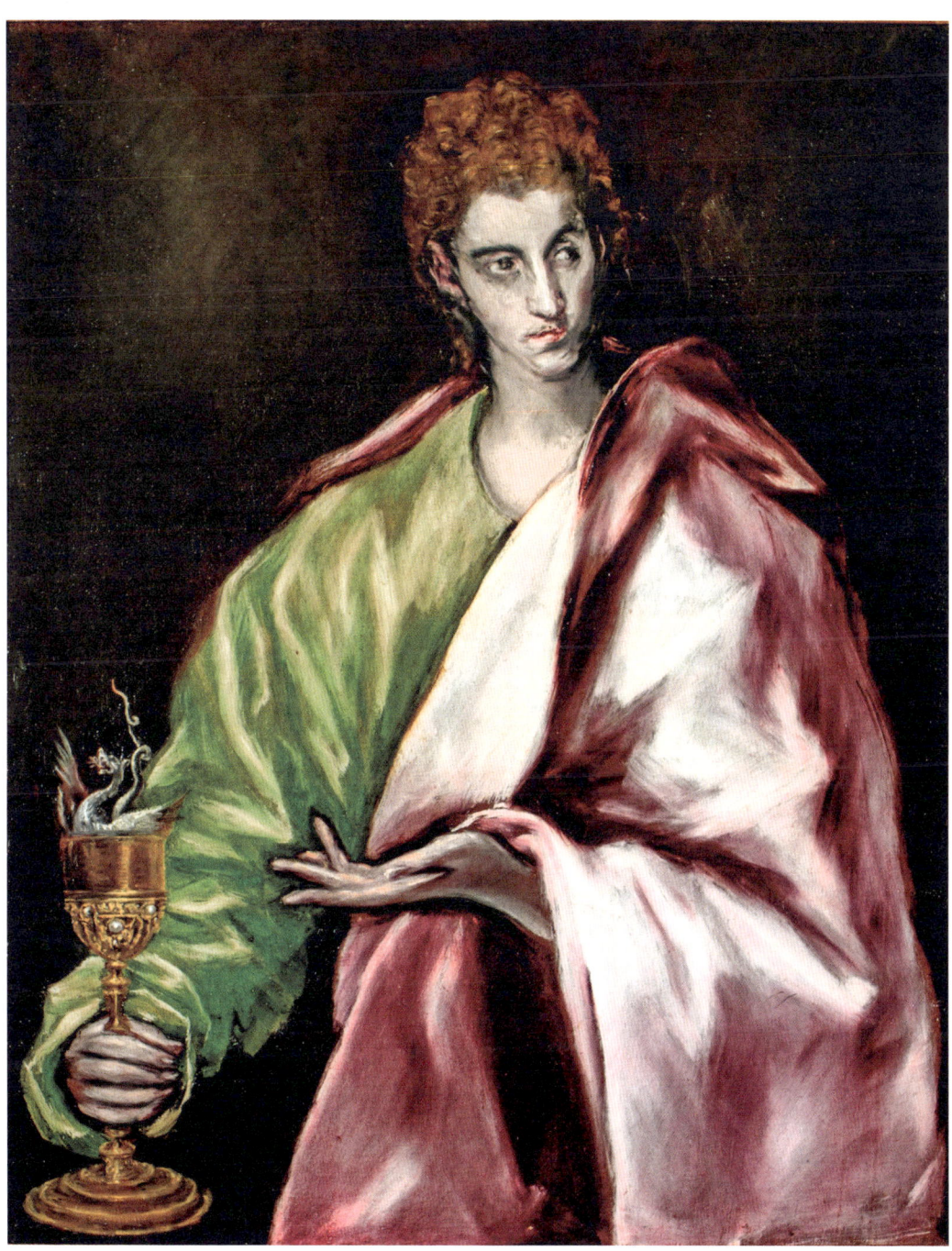

Saint John the Evangelist,
El Greco
1610-14
Oil on canvas
Museo del Prado, Madrid

Jupiter in the Guise of Diana, and the Nymph Callisto

1759

The Charm of Art

Rococo stemmed from the *rocaille* style first popularised in Italy and originating in the fashion for grottos decorated with shells and stones. During the Regency of the Duke of Orléans, etiquette at Versailles slackened and baroque made way for rococo. The fantasy, sensuality and delicacy of this new style expressed itself in bucolic scenes and sensual allegories. It waned in popularity from the 1750s onwards.

Rococo Painters

The foremost representatives of this style were Antoine Watteau, François Boucher, Jean-Marc Nattier, Jean-Honoré Fragonard and Maurice-Quentin de La Tour.

Body to Body

From 1715 onwards, libertinage flourished in Versailles society. Rooted in literary tradition, it became an unbridled quest for physical pleasures and frivolity. In art, mythology served as a ready-made pretext for sensual scenes gracing aristocratic interiors.

François Boucher was one of the artists who most excelled in this fantasist, captivating style epitomising the period, specialising in genre scenes, pastorales and allegories featuring graceful female nudes. In this picture, Boucher is indulging himself in a theme popular with rococo artists, the loves of the gods, very probably inspired by Ovid's *Metamorphoses*.

Jupiter, identifiable here by the eagle in the top righthand corner, has transformed himself into Diana, recognisable by the crescent moon on her forehead, in order to seduce the nymph Callisto. The imposter seems to have succeeded, for Callisto is languorously reclining in his arms. Such godly loves were ideal pretexts for sensual scenes and also enabled the depiction of not one but several female nudes in situations with the most licentious Sapphic overtones.

François Boucher used the pastel hues so typical of the rococo style to intensify the delicacy of a composition in which the flesh tones are heightened with pink nuances accentuating lips and nipples flushed with emotion. A shimmering sheet shelters this forbidden love yet exalts it by contrasting with the green and blue vegetation. Finally, as if an extra touch of charm were needed, plump cherubs are gazing mischievously down on the scene. The artist's aim here was to intoxicate the viewer in a pleasurable, appetising awakening of the senses.

Jupiter's gallantries are only depicted to fill
our thoughts with pleasure in a continual series
of libertine amusements.

Abbé Pluche

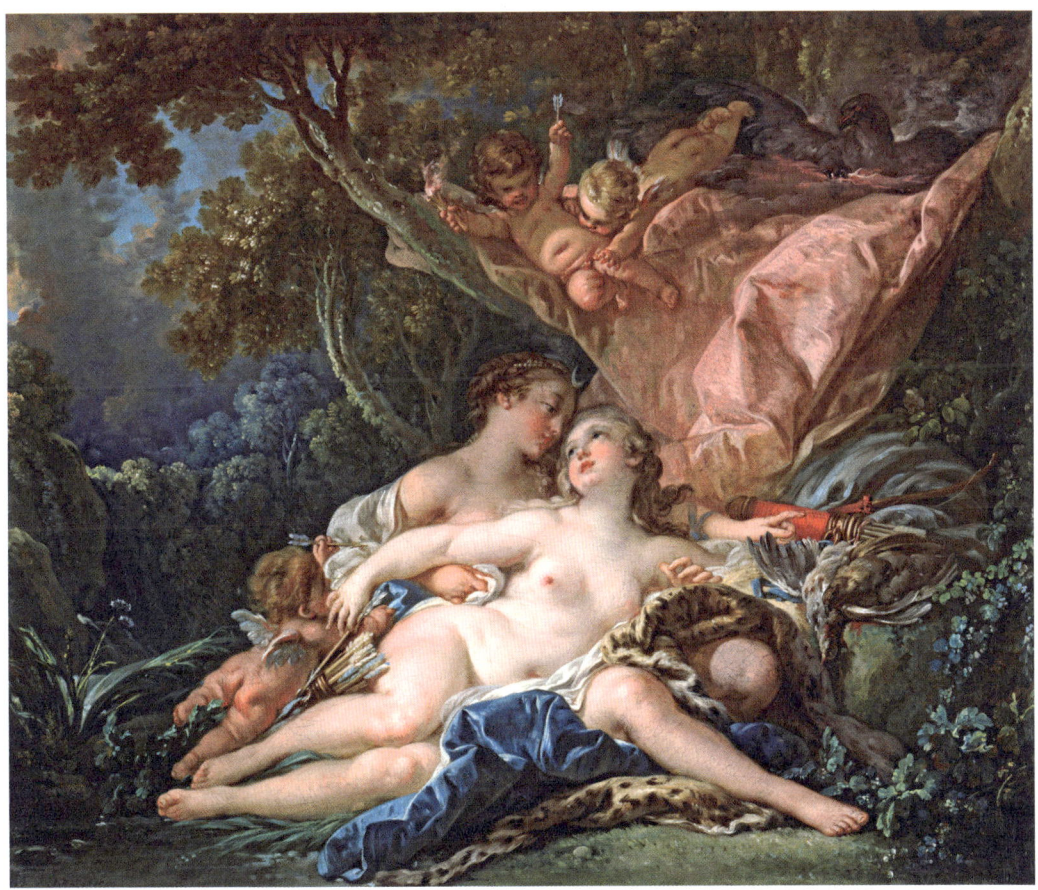

Jupiter in the Guise of Diana,
and the Nymph Callisto,
François Boucher
1759
Oil on canvas
The Nelson-Atkins Museum of Art,
Kansas City

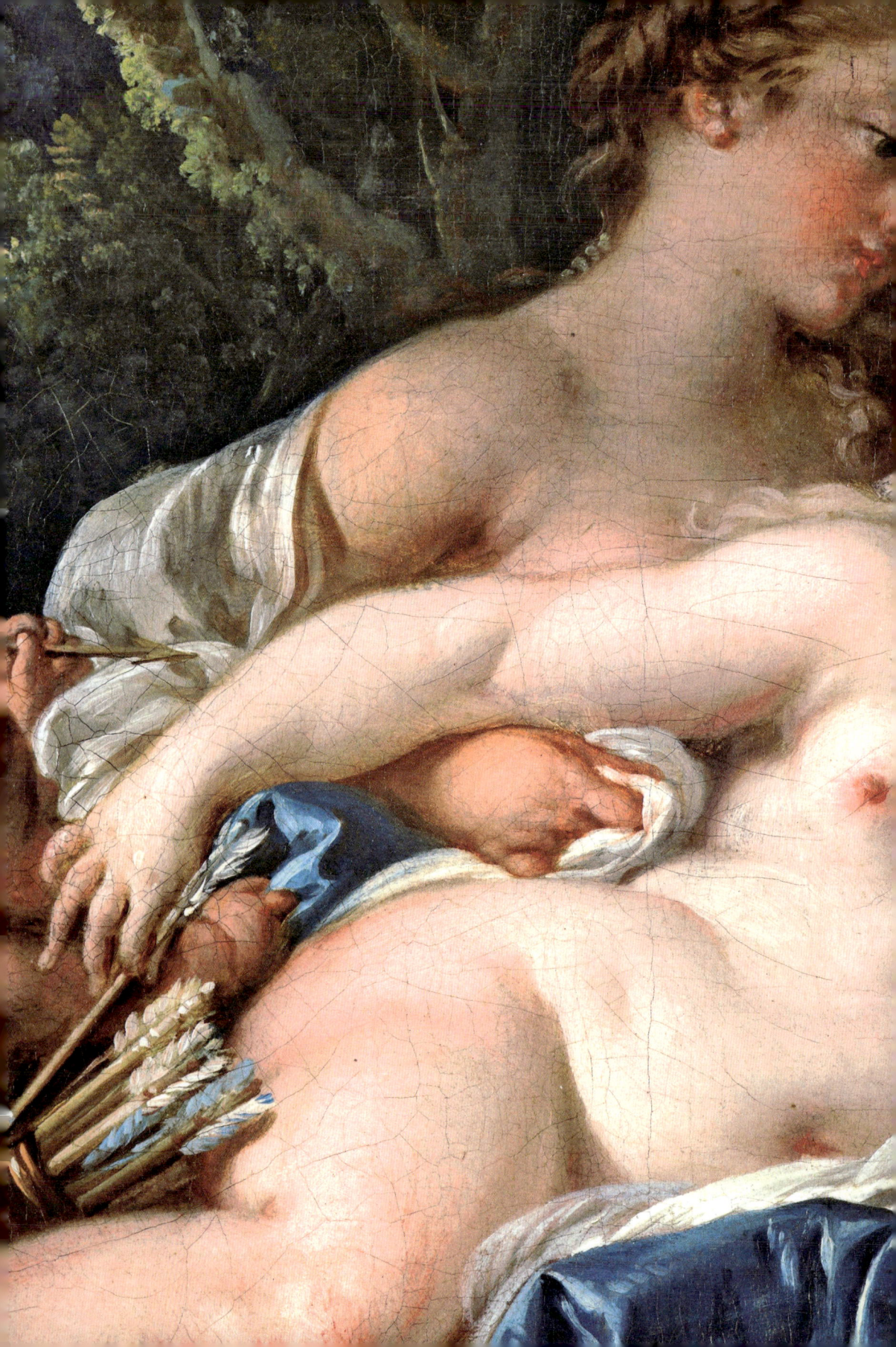

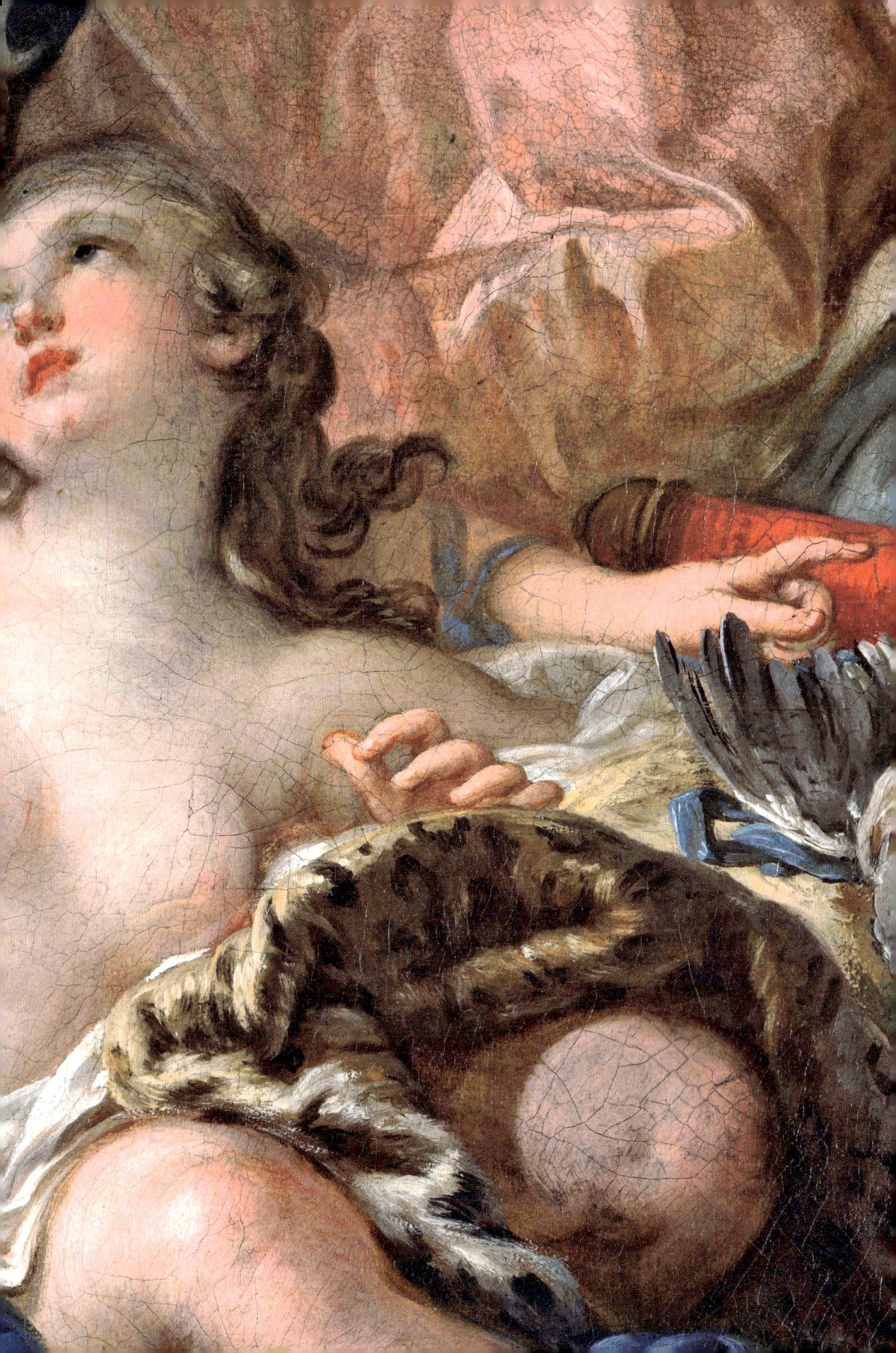

Kushi (The Comb)

1795/96

Kushi (Comb),
Kitagawa Utamaro
1795/96
Print
Library of Congress,
Washington

Woman-flower

During the Edo period, Japan saw the emergence of a prosperous urban bourgeoisie. To cater to the tastes of this new public, artists mass-produced woodblock prints known as *ukiyo-e*, 'images of the floating world'.

One of the most popular genres of this graphic art was *bijin-ga*, or pictures of 'the beauty of a woman's appearance', usually portrayals of courtesans and geishas. The painter Utamaro became renowned for his portraits of women majestically occupying the picture space in a manner hitherto reserved solely for Kabuki theatre actors.

The woman he is portraying here is holding a comb in front of her face. The comb is transparent, to not impede our admiration of the woman's features but also to draw our attention to her mouth accentuated in bright pink. Shown in front of wallpaper with a stylised floral motif heightened with mica flakes (Utamaro invented this technique), she is wearing a kimono sensually revealing the curves of her bust and her delicate neck, a highly erotic zone in Japanese culture. Her portrayal in close-up and the sparkling background accentuate the splendour of this young woman, an object of desire but also a hieratic figure. Her superb chignon creates a certain contrast between the imposing, almost geometricised volume of her jet-black hair and the finesse of the rest of her figure.

Utamaro was mingling eroticism and refinement in an image emphasising the customs of Japanese culture without neglecting nature, expressed here in the curves of the model's kimono blooming like a flower. Even if there is a concern for realism in his portraits, Utamaro transformed women into immaterial icons of fantasy and desire.

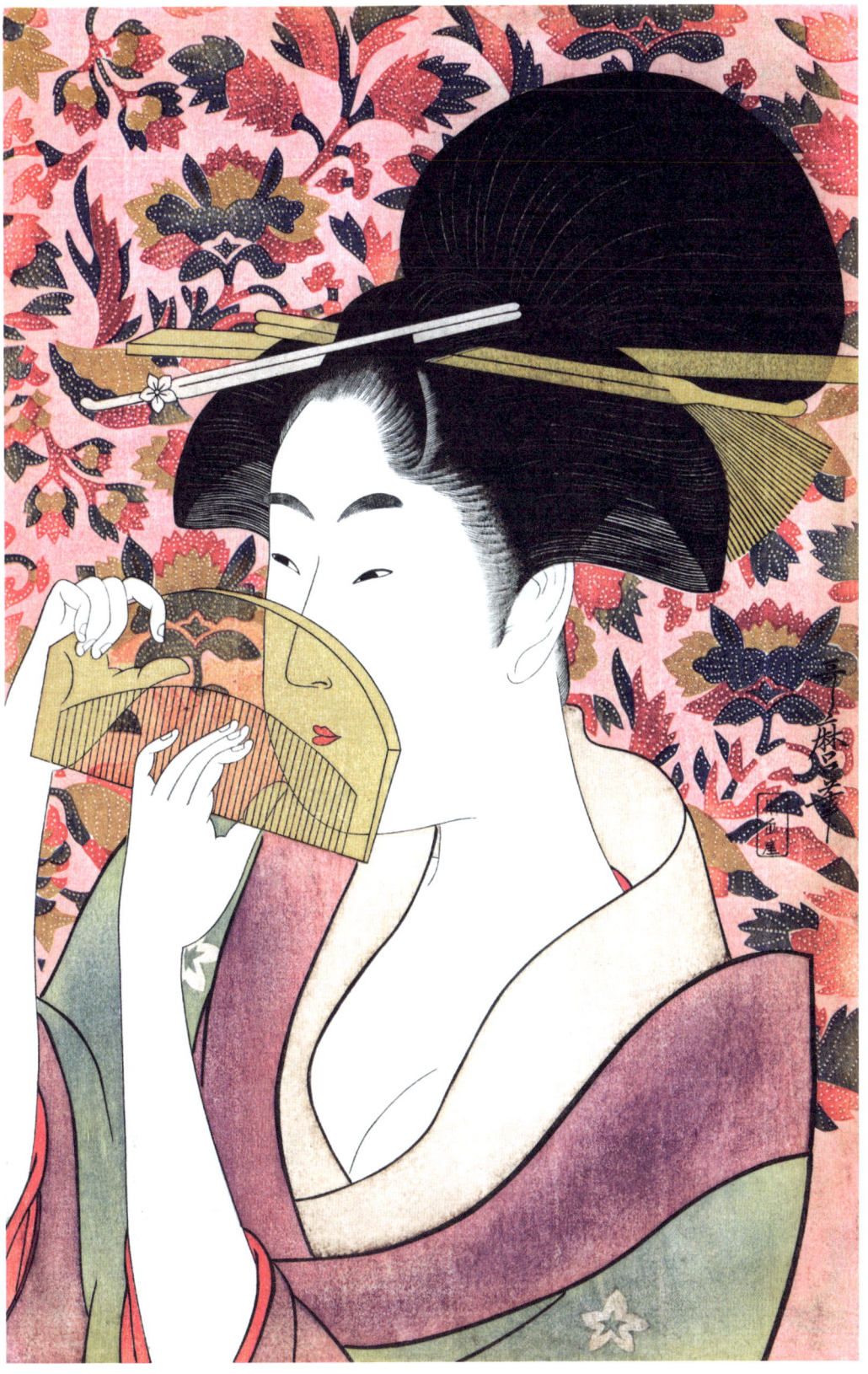

Les Hasards heureux de l'escarpolette (The Swing)

1767–69

Libertine Literature

In France, libertine transgression expressed itself in the salons and in literature from the seventeenth century onwards, in works such as Marivaux's *The Triumph of Love*, Voltaire's *L'Ingénu*, Choderlos de Laclos's *Les Liaisons Dangereuses* and the Marquis de Sade's *Justine, or the Misfortunes of Virtue*.

TIMELINE
Children's games

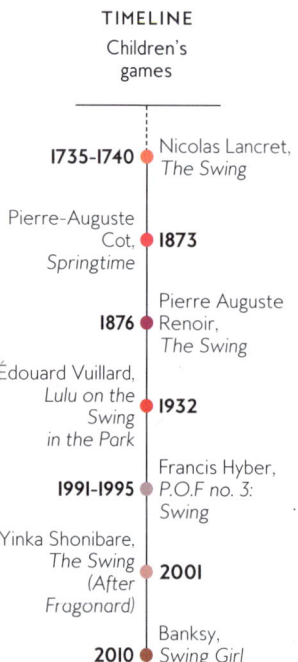

1735–1740 Nicolas Lancret, *The Swing*

Pierre-Auguste Cot, *Springtime* **1873**

1876 Pierre Auguste Renoir, *The Swing*

Édouard Vuillard, *Lulu on the Swing in the Park* **1932**

1991–1995 Francis Hyber, *P.O.F no. 3: Swing*

Yinka Shonibare, *The Swing (After Fragonard)* **2001**

2010 Banksy, *Swing Girl*

Licentious Games

In 1767 François-David Bollioud de Saint-Julien, Baron of Argental, wanted to commission a picture portraying his mistress. He approached the painter Gabriel-François Doyen with a clear idea in mind.

The baron wanted the young woman to be sitting 'on a swing being pushed by a bishop. You will place me in such a way that I am able to see the legs of this beautiful child, and even more if you wish to further enliven your picture'. The artist was embarrassed by the baron's stipulations, which he considered frivolous, so it was Jean-Honoré Fragonard who executed the commission instead. Although no stranger to licentious subjects, to avoid accusations of anticlericalism Fragonard preferred to replace the bishop with a cuckold husband.

Against a backdrop of luxuriant vegetation, a young woman on a swing is being pushed by her deceived husband, while another man reclining beneath the seductress is admiring the sight above him. Yes, she may well have deliberately let her shoe drop, erotically revealing her ankle, but one wonders whether she is showing a little more . . . In any case, the admirer seems excited by the vision above him because he has fallen back into the flowers. Fragonard has caught the alluring woman in a ray of sunlight also illuminating her lover's admiring face, while the ridiculed husband is in the shade.

The artist has adorned the object of the young man's desire in a flouncy, sparkling pink that heightens the sensuality of this moment and implicates us as equally mischievous accomplices in the deceit taking place before our eyes. The sculpture of a cherub with a finger held to his lips seems to be telling us to say not a word.

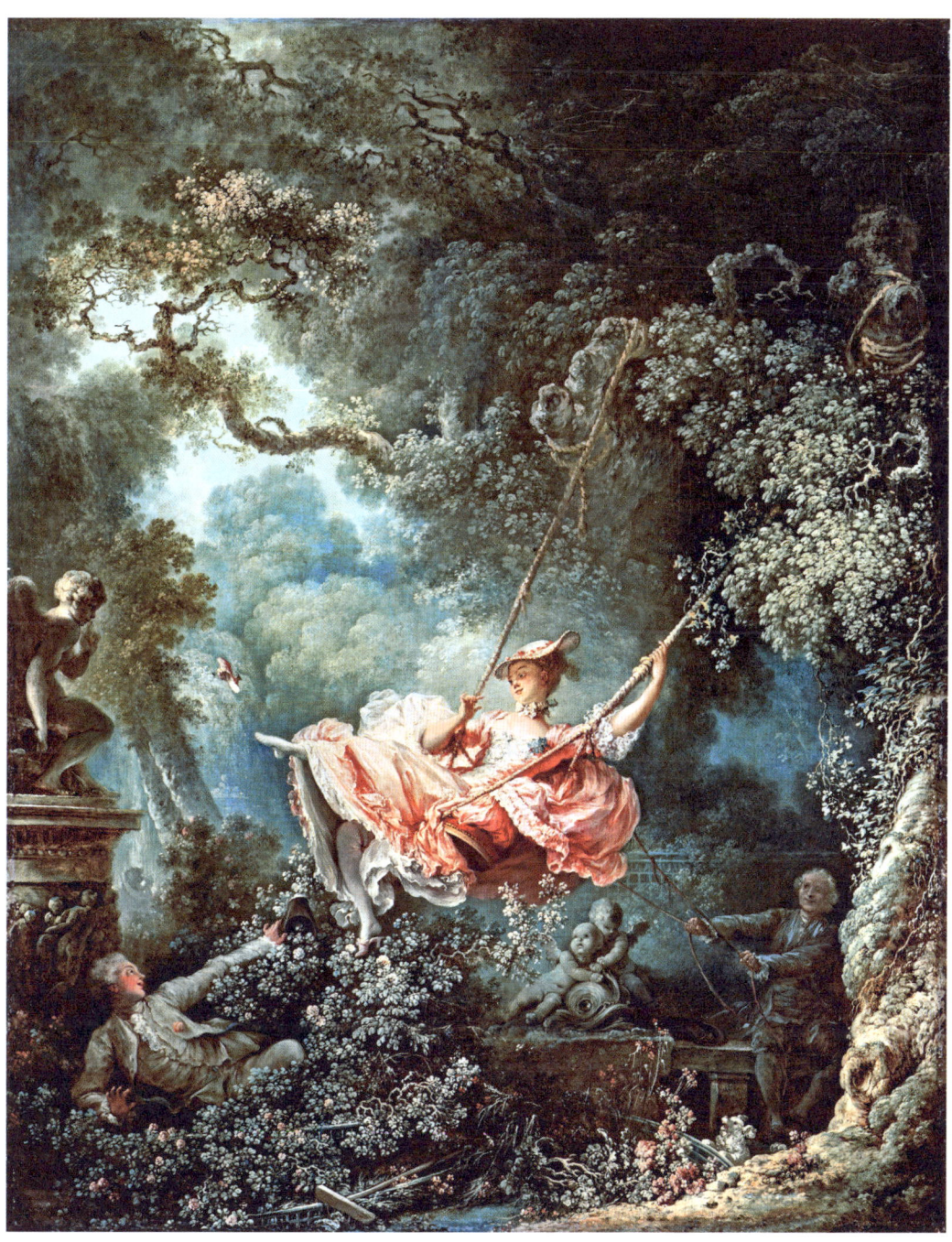

Les Hasards heureux de l'escarpolette
(The Swing),
Jean-Honoré Fragonard
1767–69
Oil on canvas
Wallace Collection, London

Ballet

1876

Behind the Scenes

Ballet at the Paris Opéra was a major source of inspiration for Edgar Degas, because there he could study both the dancers' movements and a backstage world in a late nineteenth-century society invigorated by the Industrial Revolution.

Degas' focus here is on the ballerina, the principal dancer of the corps de ballet, performing an arabesque as she advances alone across the stage. The plunging viewpoint, probably from a box, accentuates the ballerina's upper body and her graceful gestures. She is bathed in a brilliant light that confuses the whiteness of her skin and the delicate pink tones of her tutu.

It is she who has all our attention because the rest of the picture - the stage set, the other dancers waiting their turn and the man in black - is only roughly sketched in. Degas was intent on showing us both the dream and its dark side. The dancer is portrayed like a flower, haloed by her vaporous corolla, but in her pink cheeks he is also showing the physical effort and strain required to create such an entrancing spectacle. He contrasts this enchanting figure with the tumult and chaotic colours in the background and the rather ominous, lurking figure of the man.

Degas is emphasising the less glamorous underside of classical dance. Wealthy spectators could go backstage, watch rehearsals and therefore observe dancers in their intimacy. And as they often came from humble backgrounds they needed a 'protector' to practice their art, and so there developed a pernicious system of prostitution. The hidden side of the dream . . .

A Unique Print

Here Degas used monotype, a technique enabling one to print an image drawn or painted on a sheet of glass or metal (copper or zinc in Degas' case) coated with ink. Unlike an etching, which can be printed many times, a monotype can be reproduced only once. Degas then heightened this monotype with pastel.

I Was There

'Having seen the pastels you no longer need to go to the Opera,' the critic Georges Rivière wrote after visiting the third Impressionist exhibition.

Ballet,
Edgar Degas
1876
Pastel on monotype
Musée d'Orsay, Paris

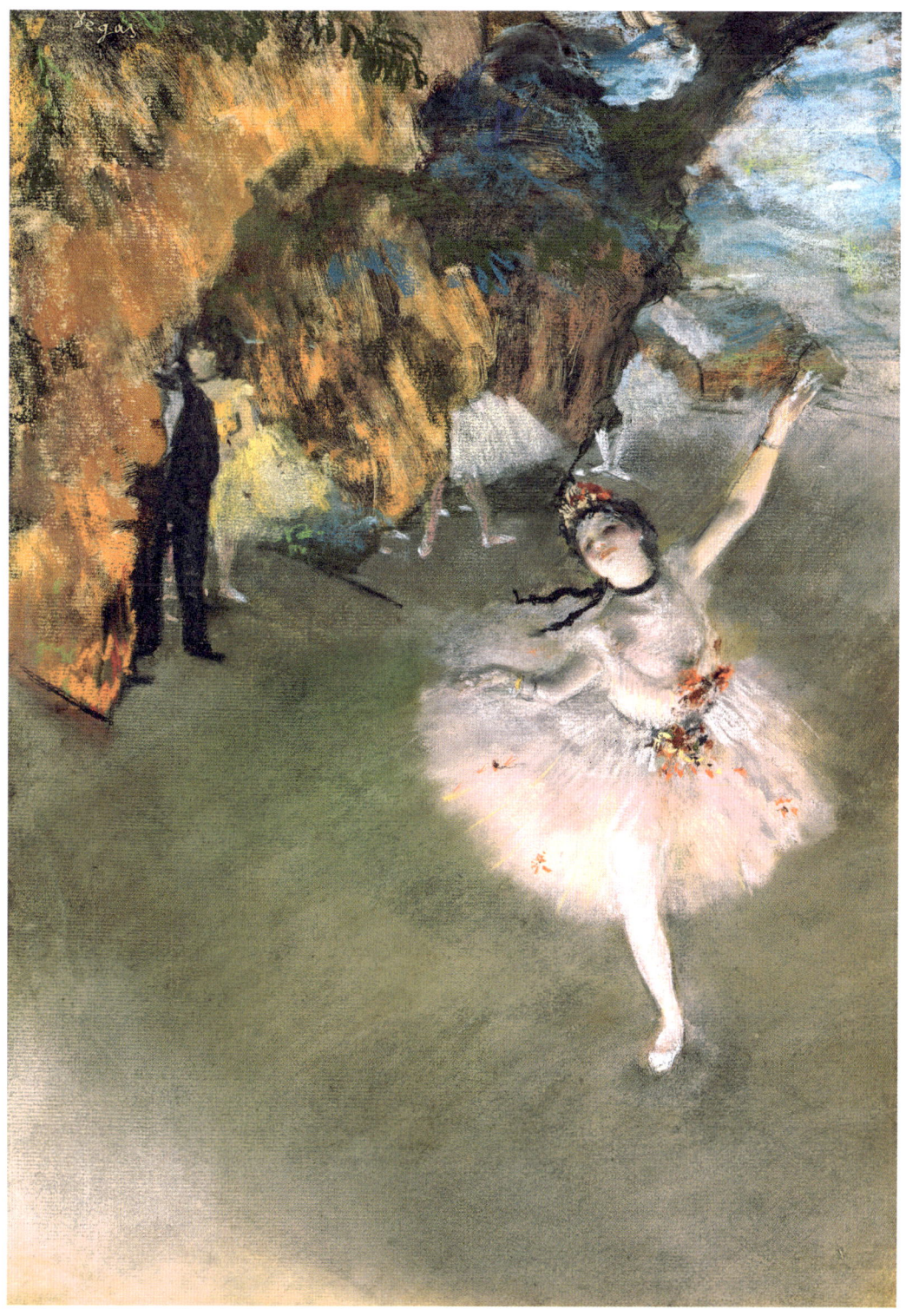

Sunset on the Seine at Lavacourt, Winter Effect

1880

Winter Day by Day

In 1872 Claude Monet painted Impression, Sunrise, the seminal work that heralded the birth of Impressionism and even modern art. He went on to paint several series of pictures dematerialising nature, its cycles and seasons.

In September 1878 Monet and his family went to live on the banks of the Seine at Vétheuil near Paris. In front of his house, from his boat-studio moored at the bottom of his garden, he could observe the village of Lavacourt. When snow and cold paralysed the locality in the winter of 1879–80, he painted some twenty pictures recording the thaw on the river. As was his habit, Monet attentively observed these metrological phenomena, painting the sensationally harsh winter from day to day.

Lavacourt and the Seine are shown here in the setting sun. Nature, highlighted in darker touches of paint, is present in the form of the small islands in front of the faintly visible village, almost dissolved in the blue distance. This horizon line divides sky and water, linked in a melancholic harmony of pink light. Into this absolute calm, Claude Monet adds life and movement in the form of the wavelets speckling the river and the boats with their passengers. Everything is shrouded in a cold mist, warmed only by the orange sun descending beyond the village, its reflections glinting in the water.

Juxtaposing his rapid brushstrokes, Monet hurriedly crystalised this unique light before the sun finally set.

I want to paint the air in which the bridge,
house or boat exists. The beauty of the air where
they are. Yet it is nothing short of impossible.

Claude Monet

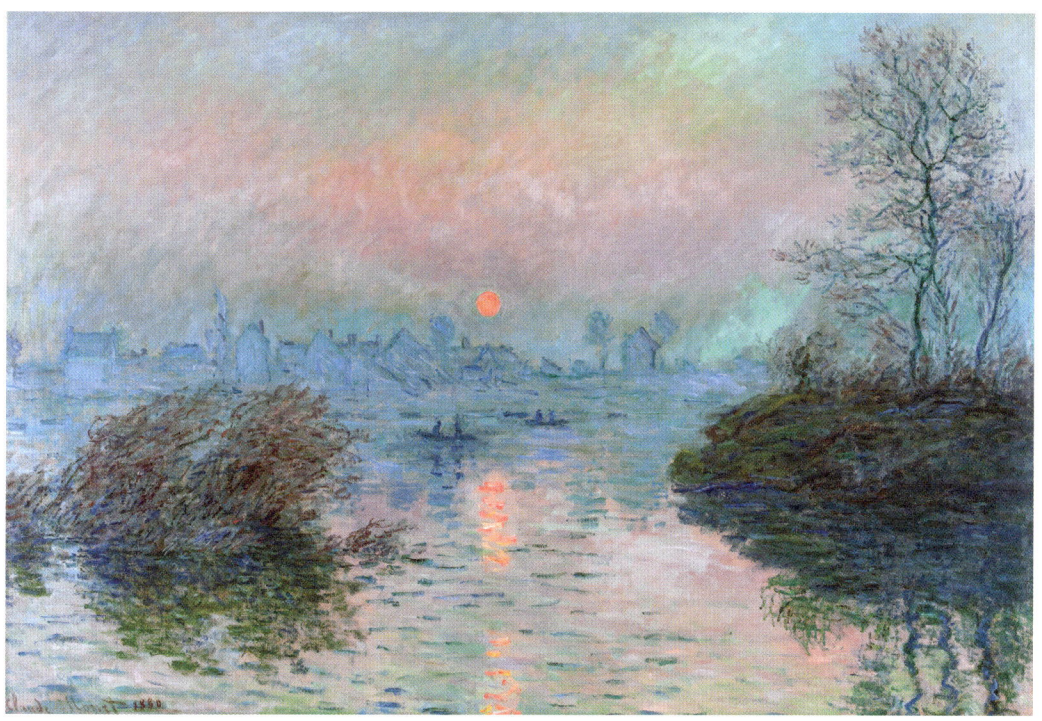

Sunset on the Seine at
Lavacourt, Winter Effect,
Claude Monet
1880
Oil on canvas
Petit Palais, Paris

L'Ambitieuse (Political Woman)

1883-85

And Fashion Created Woman

James Tissot made female dress a central subject, as an element contextualising his paintings and also as a focus of his pictorial and narrative concerns.

From 1883 to 1885 he painted a series of fifteen pictures titled *La Femme à Paris*. In these portraits, he is inviting us to observe the workings of the society of his time and above all women's role in it. Because even if her role was regarded as secondary, outside the political and economic world she was not completely ignored. But with the advent of the Belle Epoque at the end of the century, women became fantasised, mythicized, outrageously eroticised femmes fatales.

So what woman is Tissot portraying here? Who is this elegant creature in pink? For him she is 'L'Ambitieuse', but he adds 'Political Woman'. But in the context of the period, 'political' would certainly have meant 'social'.

So, a 'social woman', a socialite? This certainly seems to be what she would like to be, the centre of attention in her rustling, flouncy outfit. We sense that her dress is being worn for a purpose, so that she will be noticed and, yes, more rapidly climb the social ladder. But at that time there was no shortage of demi-mondaines, women seeking a wealthy protector to help them find fortune in high society. Often they had no choice: it was that or nothing.

Curiosity

When Tissot began his series of pictures, Zola had just published *Au Bonheur des Dames*. Both were intrigued by fashion and the ways in which it affects the life of women in society.

Tissot knew this and merely observes her without judging her. He is showing the effort she is making. Her dress is a protagonist in its own right, there to make her stand out amidst all these men in black. She may seem superficial but she is only playing the role she has been allotted. She is a frivolous, clever, seductive, ambitious woman.

L'Ambitieuse (Femme politique),
James Tissot
1883-85
Oil on canvas
Albright-Knox Art Gallery, Buffalo

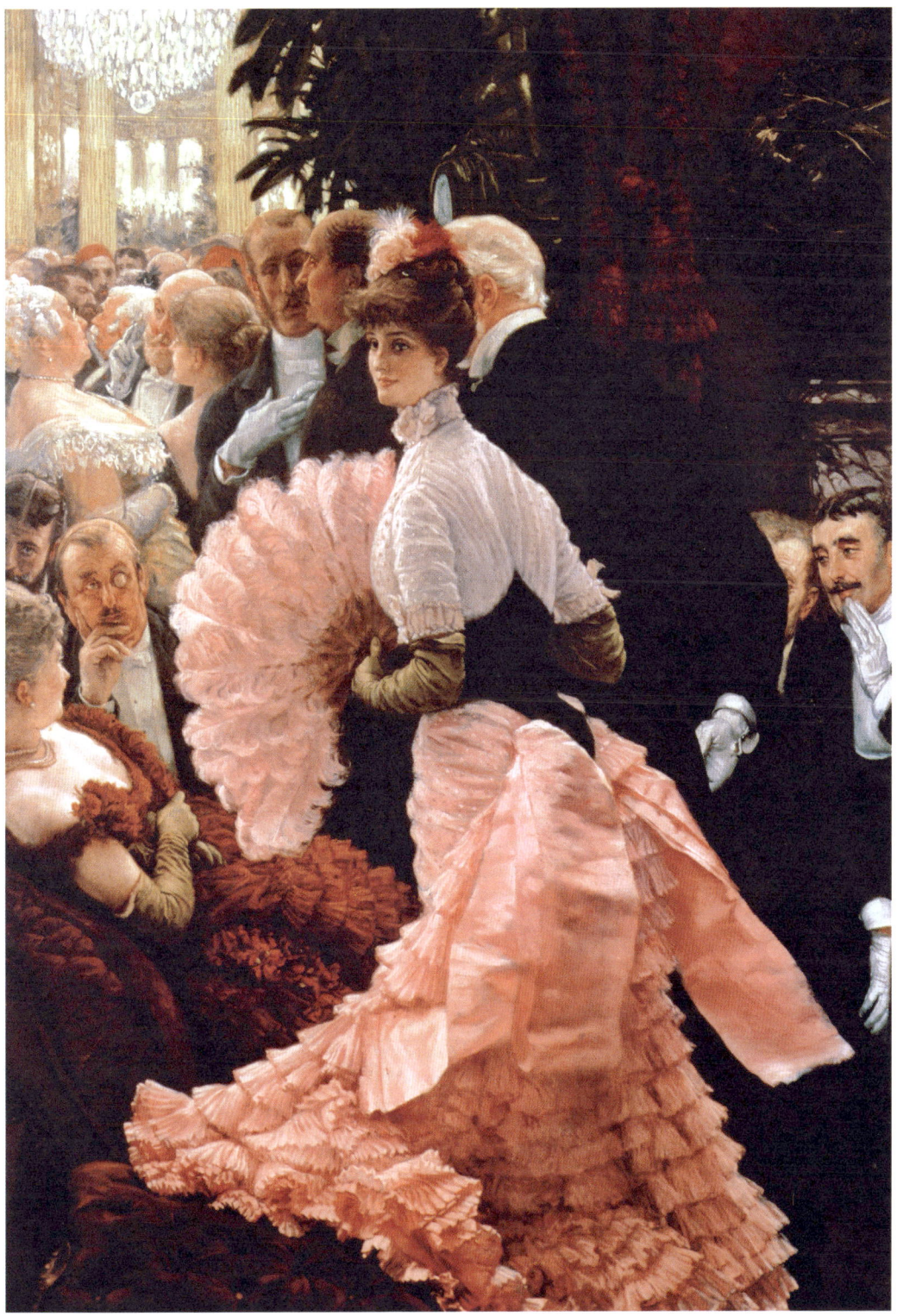

The Roses of Heliogabalus

1888

Flower Deliveries

Rumour has it that because roses were not in season in England at the time Alma-Tadema had rose petals delivered from the South of France over a four-month period in order to paint this picture.

The Taste for the Beautiful

———

Like Dante Gabriel Rossetti, James Abbott McNeill Whistler and Edwards Burne-Jones, Alma-Tadema reflects an aesthetic tendency that developed in Great Britain in the late nineteenth century, close to the Arts & Crafts movement initiated by William Morris. The aim of these 'Pre-Raphaelite' artists was to create 'art for art's sake', to privilege beauty and the awakening of the senses rather than narrative or practical concerns.

Showering Roses

The Dutchman Lawrence Alma-Tadema discovered Italy and the ruins at Pompeii during his honeymoon in 1863. His virtuoso depictions of antique architecture in his grandiose compositions earned him the nickname 'the painter of marble'.

Despite his short-lived reign, the Roman emperor Heliogabalus became infamous for his scandalous, orgy-filled life of luxury. Here Lawrence Alma-Tadema is depicting a fictive episode in his life, a banquet during which he is supposed to have murdered his guests by burying them with rose petals. A death by asphyxia that begins like a dream with the flowers cascading down from the ceiling, perfuming the air with their heady scent.

Successive moments seem to be depicted here: on the right figures are delighting in the shower of roses, while on the left the scene is more violent with figures trying to escape from the smothering petals. The emperor, reclining in a golden tunic, and his guests look on unmoved, admiring this both morbid and deliciously romantic spectacle.

This perversely ambivalent scene can be seen as a sharp criticism of the Victorian society in which Alma-Tadema lived. The original text describes a shower of violets but he preferred to depict roses, a symbol of luxury in England. One should also recall that the nation was then a powerful empire which, claiming moralising and civilising motives, colonised territories with arrogant supremacy. Alma-Tadema is showing the hypocrisy of a system which, feigning integrity, smothers its subjects with sufficiency and points its finger at hedonism as the great enemy to better divert our attention.

The Roses of Heliogabalus,
Lawrence Alma-Tadema
1888
Oil on canvas
Private collection

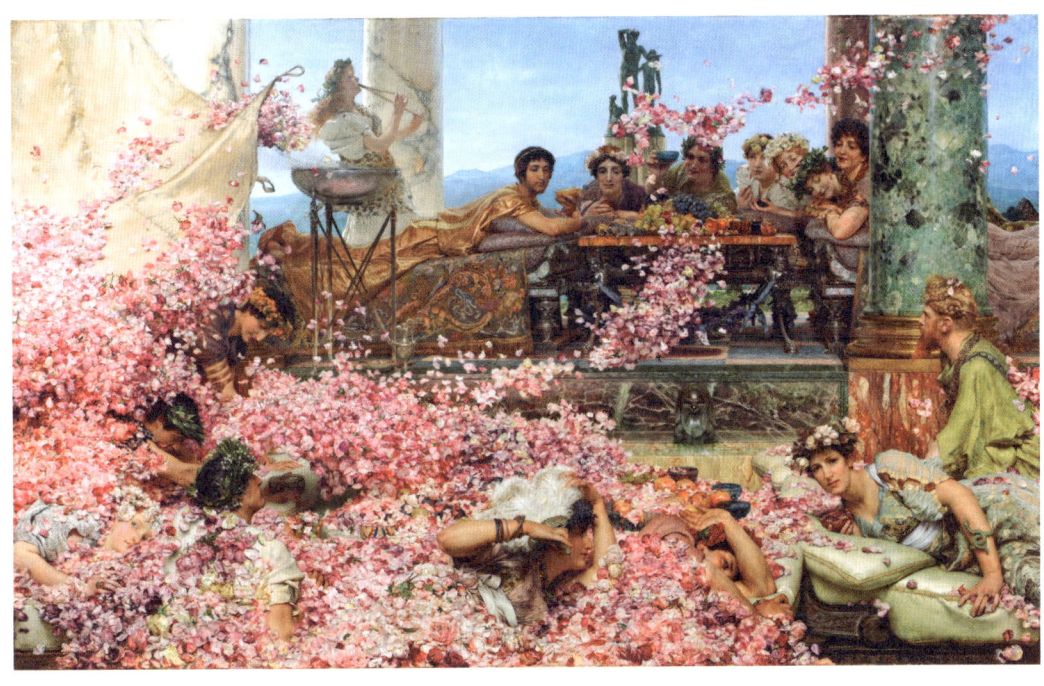

Life is a rose whose every petal is an allusion and each thorn is a reality.

Alfred de Musset

Tahitian Women on the Beach

1891

Women as Objects

When Paul Gauguin settled in Tahiti in 1891 he wanted to live a life of ecstasy, calm and art. He painted the island's colourful landscapes and seemingly primitive lifestyle in complete daily harmony with nature.

Since his stay at Pont-Aven in Brittany, he had developed a symbolist style in his works composed of areas of flat colour and synthetic forms. Tahiti nourished this new taste, enabling Gauguin to free himself from traditional pictorial rules to depict a culture into which he could project his own imagination and fantasies.

He had only just arrived on the island and was discovering, contemplating and trying to understand it. The most everyday sights intrigued him, such as these two women going about their daily tasks. Portraying them in close-up, he gave them a grandiose, massive, hieratic, impassive presence. Yet there is not the slightest heaviness, only the gentleness of their curved outlines, the elegant floral motifs and the delicate pink of the dress of the woman on the right.

A pink which conveys a certain melancholy and one wonders whether Gauguin also noted this delicate colour's ambivalent quality. Gauguin is depicting the languor of the islanders, a listlessness composed of melancholy and spirituality. He compounds the nonchalance of their gestures with their stoic, timeless expressions, making them more objects of study than subjects. This is the inquisitive eye of a white man, of a foreign civilisation intruding and imposing itself, as shown by the European dress recalling the colonialist missionaries that arrived from the eighteenth century to convert these distant lands.

Maturity

In Dresden there is another version of this picture, painted in 1892 and entitled *Parau Api*, in which Gauguin replaced the pink dress with a pareo or sarong. Had the artist understood that he no longer had to act as an anthropologist but as a fellow islander?

An Esoteric Art

The literary and artistic movement known as Symbolism began in 1876 when Émile Zola described the work of Gustave Moreau as 'symbolist'. In the idealist yet pessimist symbolism of their work, artists, poets and writers such as Gustav Klimt, Odilon Redon, Gustave Moreau, Fernand Khnopff, James Ensor, Stéphane Mallarmé and Joris-Karl Huysmans showed their preoccupation with chimera, the spiritual and the subconscious.

In matters of art one's state of mind is three-quarters of what counts, so it has to be carefully nurtured if you want to do something great and lasting.

Paul Gauguin

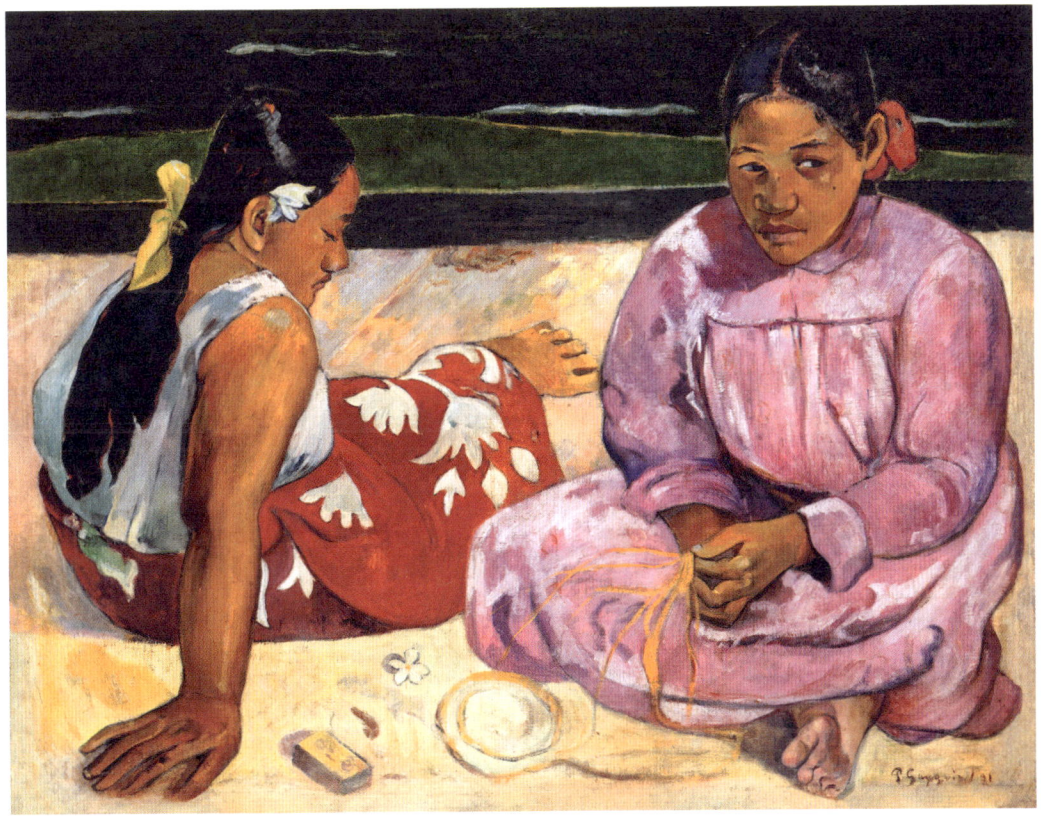

Tahitian Women on the Beach,
Paul Gauguin
1891
Oil on canvas
Musée d'Orsay, Paris

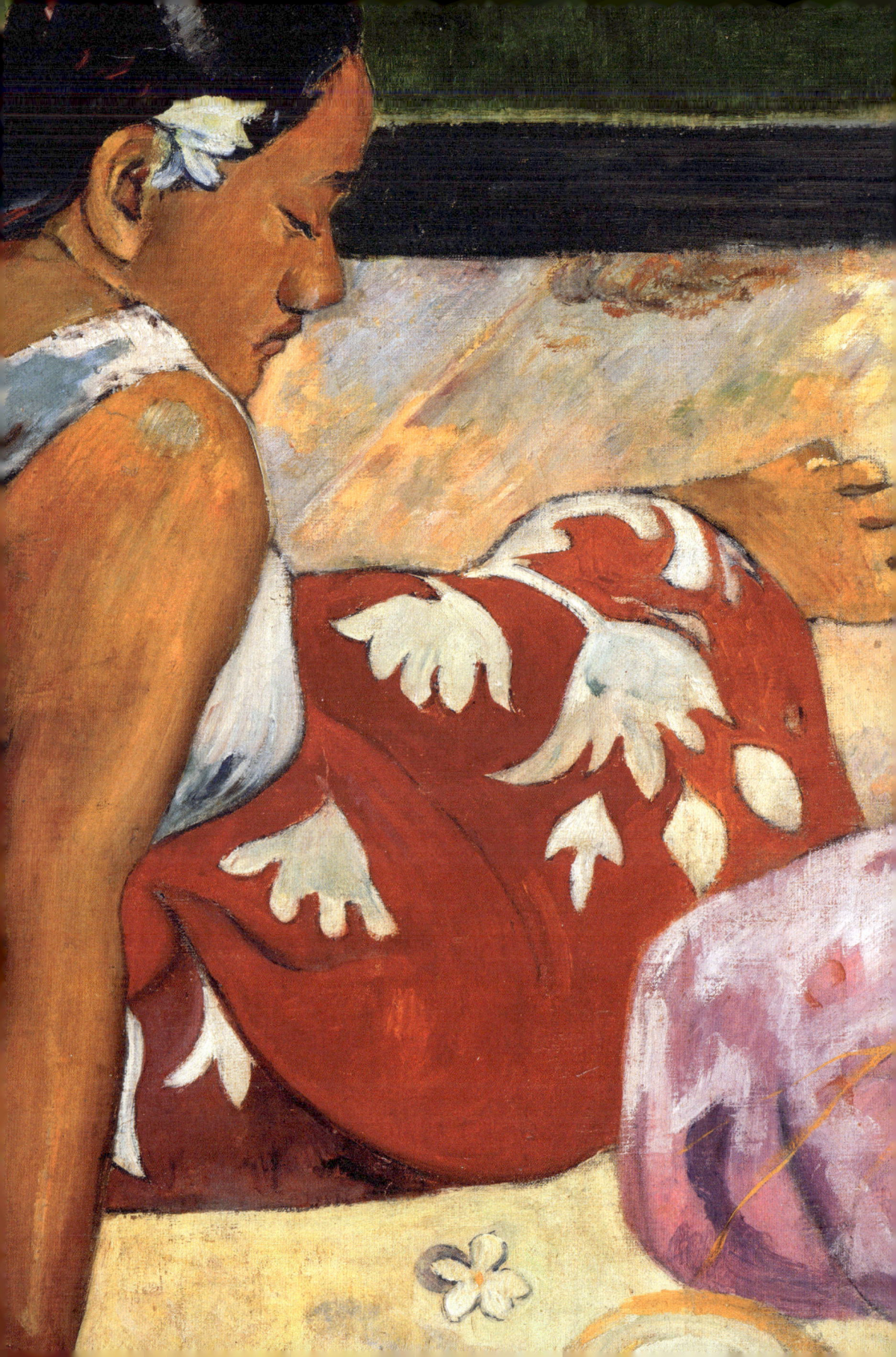

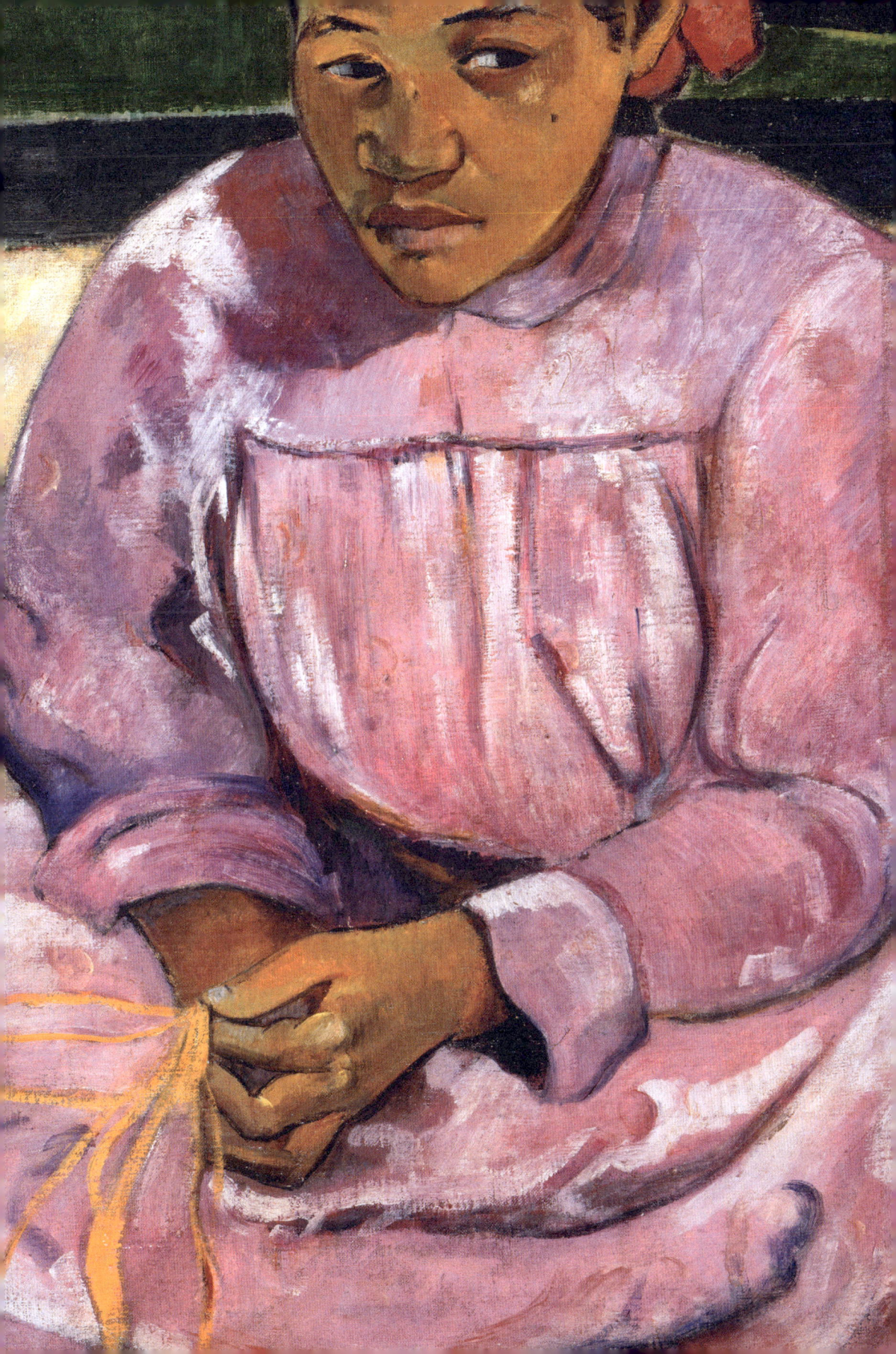

Les Demoiselles d'Avignon

1907

Geolocation

These young ladies have nothing to do with the Papal City of Avignon. Picasso is paying tribute to the prostitutes in a street in Barcelona, the Carrer d'Avinyó. He even wanted to call the picture *El Burdel de Aviñón*, but his picture dealer objected.

Cubism

Les Demoiselles d'Avignon is generally regarded as Cubism's founding work yet in parallel Picasso and Braque were both already geometricising reality before they began working closely together in 1908. Other prominent members of the movement were Juan Gris, Albert Gleizes, Jean Metzinger, Marcel Duchamp and Fernand Léger.

An Artistic Outrage

At the beginning of the twentieth century the art world was in turmoil. Norms and conventions were being deconstructed by aesthetic movements experimenting with abstraction. Depicting reality was no longer an absolute aim.

Pablo Picasso spent long hours producing countless studies, altering a face here, a group of figures there before finally painting one of the seminal works of modern art, representing a group of women in a way that no one had previously dared to do. The five demoiselles gazing at us, seemingly hacked into shape with a pruning hook, are depicted both in profile and frontally, their features reminiscent of the Iberian sculpture and primal African art then very fashionable in avant-garde Parisian circles.

The women are sensual and voluptuous, naked but not denuded in the classical manner. Their bodies have been reduced to geometric forms and areas of flat colour almost resembling collage.

The picture was rejected by the critics and public because Picasso was depicting the hallowed subject of the female nude, even apparently deforming the faces of the two demoiselles on the right with symptoms of syphilis. The still life with fruit at their feet is another departure from classicism. Yet Pablo Picasso is stressing that these are definitely female nudes by colouring them flesh-tinted pink.

In his preparatory studies, Picasso had intended to include two men in the scene, but finally preferred to have these majestic, proud women entirely occupy the composition.

Les Demoiselles d'Avignon,
Pablo Picasso
1907
Oil on wood
Museum of Modern Art,
New York

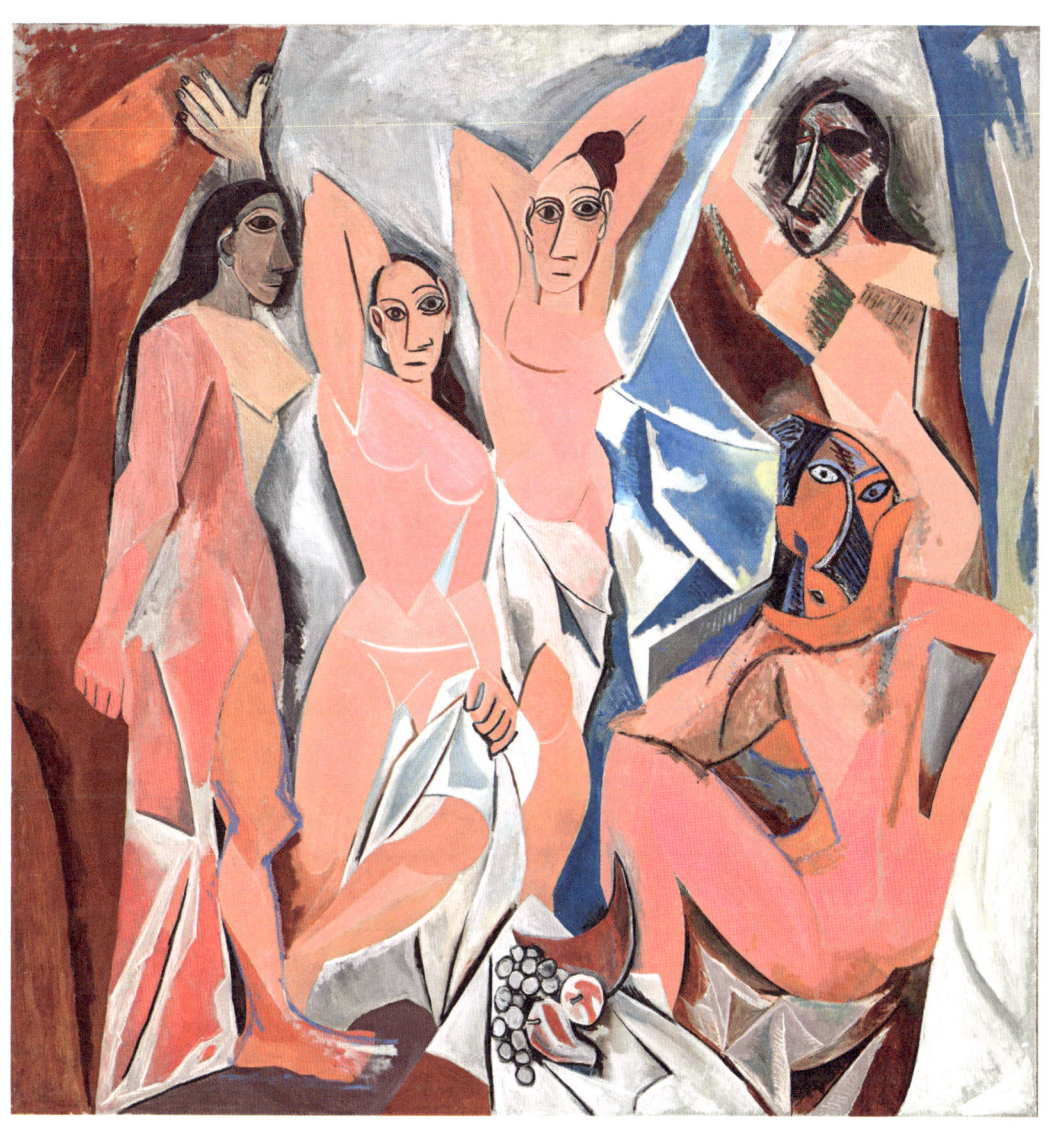

Les Demoiselles d'Avignon is the key event of the beginning of the twentieth century.

André Breton

Antibes, The Pink Cloud

1916

By the seaside

In the late 1880s the artists Georges Seurat and Paul Signac developed and theorised the Pointillist technique, in which colours are not mixed on the palette but optically by the eye.

In this seascape Paul Signac preferred large touches of paint unifying the composition's different tonalities, contrasting or complementing them and leaving the viewer to appreciate their harmonies and rhythms. The vivid shades of blue and pink unify sea and sky and the headland on the right. But the dominant element is the towering pink mass, modelled by mauve, orange and yellow tints, reflected in the water. This imposing, almost monstrous pink cloud gives the impression that it will engulf both land and sea.

Yet, despite the threatening cloud, the overall impression is one of calm. No longer surprised, our memories return. We remember skies bathed in pink on summer evenings and, overcome by a delectable torpor, watching the sun setting in the sea. It is still hot but night is about to fall, one of those furtive moments of silence before the excitement of the evening.

Paul Signac's prime subject here is light and 'colour for colour's sake' because he knows that we are creatures of emotions and memories and sometimes in a picture we only need an impression to create an entire story for ourselves. That his cloud is realistically depicted matters less than the sensations it awakens in us. A tentacular cloud more benevolent than it might seem.

Is an artist not someone who strives to create unity within variety by the rhythm of his colours and tones and who puts science at the service of his sensations?

Paul Signac

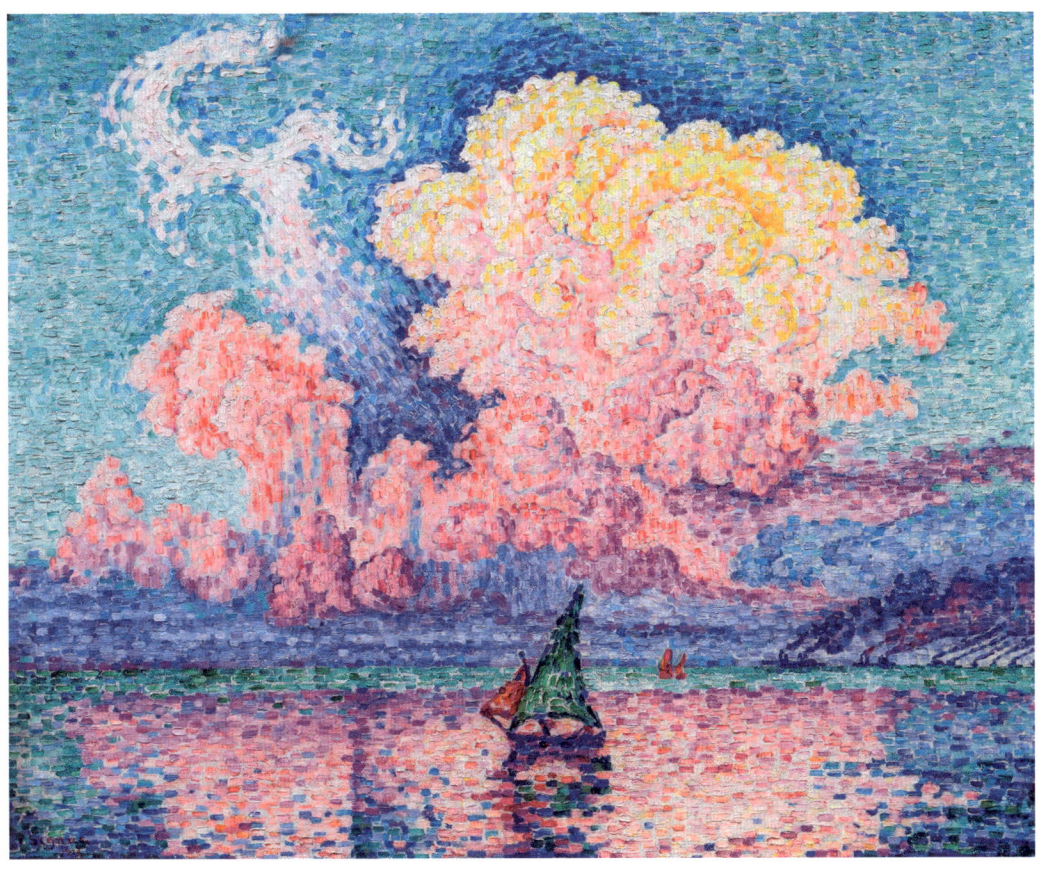

Antibes, The Pink Cloud,
Paul Signac
1916
Oil on canvas
Private collection

Thirty Years or La Vie en rose

1931

Optimistically Aging

Jack of All Trades

With Paul Poiret, Raoul Dufy founded the printed textiles company La Petite Usine. From 1912 to 1928 he worked with the Lyon silk manufacturer Bianchini-Férier, producing some four thousand designs for furnishing and fashion fabrics. He also designed decors for the passenger liner Normandie and the Théâtre de Chaillot in Paris.

The Language of Roses

——

Red: passionate love
Pink: tenderness
Orange: desire
White: purity
Yellow: friendship

While working on textile designs with the couturier Paul Poiret, Raoul Dufy developed a freer, more fanciful style in which arabesques and colour began to play an essential role.

Intent on exploring the decorative arts and crafts just as much as painting, he resolutely refused any distinction between these differing fields of creation. His innate curiosity prompted the decorative style in his paintings that inevitably evokes Henri Matisse's interiors.

As Raoul Dufy said himself and demonstrated in his work, he 'saw life in pink'. This picture, painted for a friend's thirtieth birthday, immerses us in different nuances of pink and flowers.

The composition is unified by a very light pink and articulated by the central vase of flowers on the pedestal table and the vase of flowers in the picture on the wall, only half visible and with a geometrically patterned frame. To this Dufy added a floral-patterned wallpaper. All these forms mingle, echo and compete with one another, confusing somewhat our reading of the picture but not tiring us. On the contrary, we are elated by this whirlwind of roses.

After all, what could be more joyful than a birthday? Yet for some, birthdays can be melancholic occasions. So Dufy is reassuring his friend, reminding him that life is beautiful and deserves to be celebrated, that all this pink is not only the gentlest gift but a message of hope for his young thirty-year-old friend.

Conceive as an artist and execute as a craftsman.

Raoul Dufy

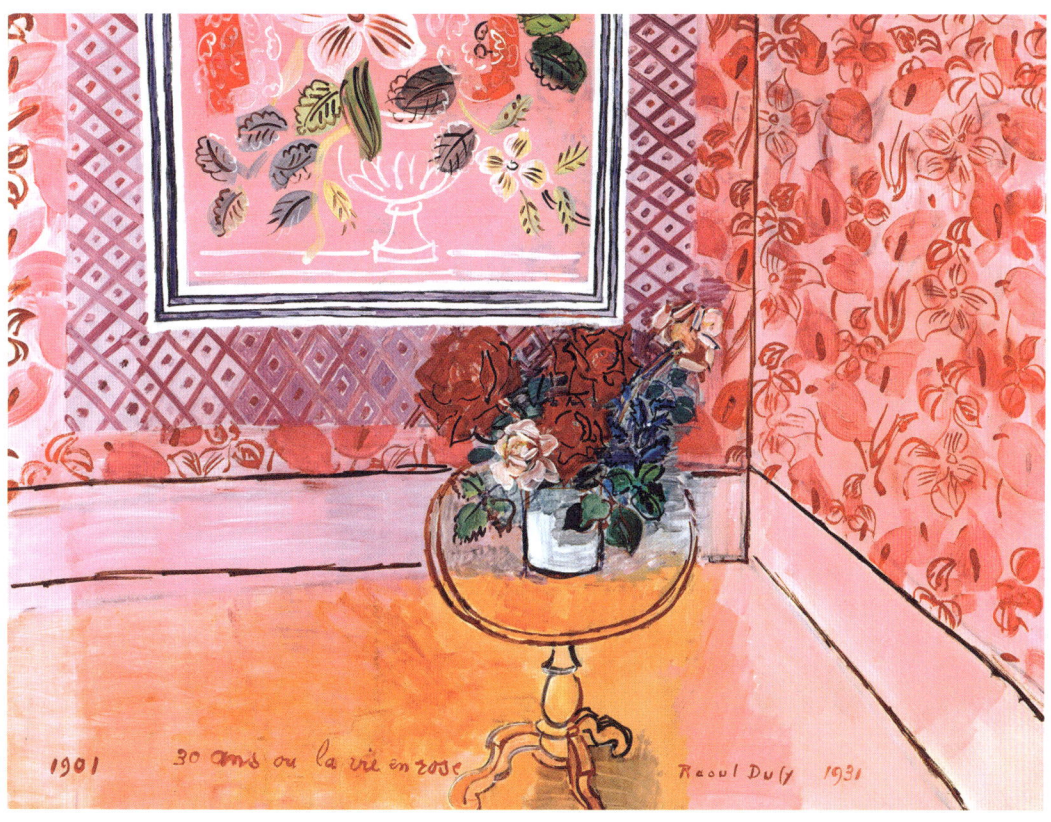

Thirty Years or La Vie en Rose,
Raoul Dufy
1931
Oil on canvas
Musée d'Art moderne de Paris

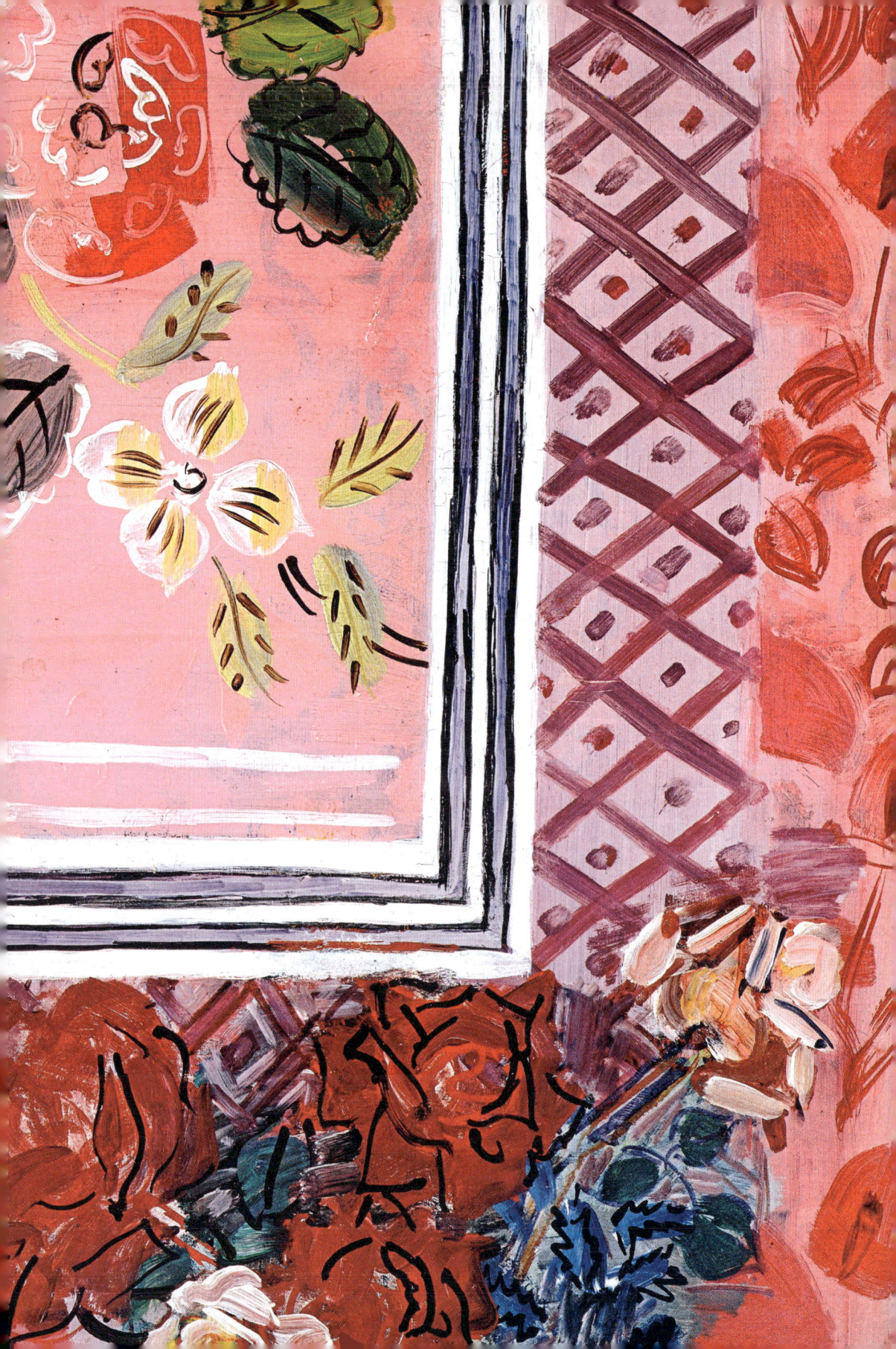

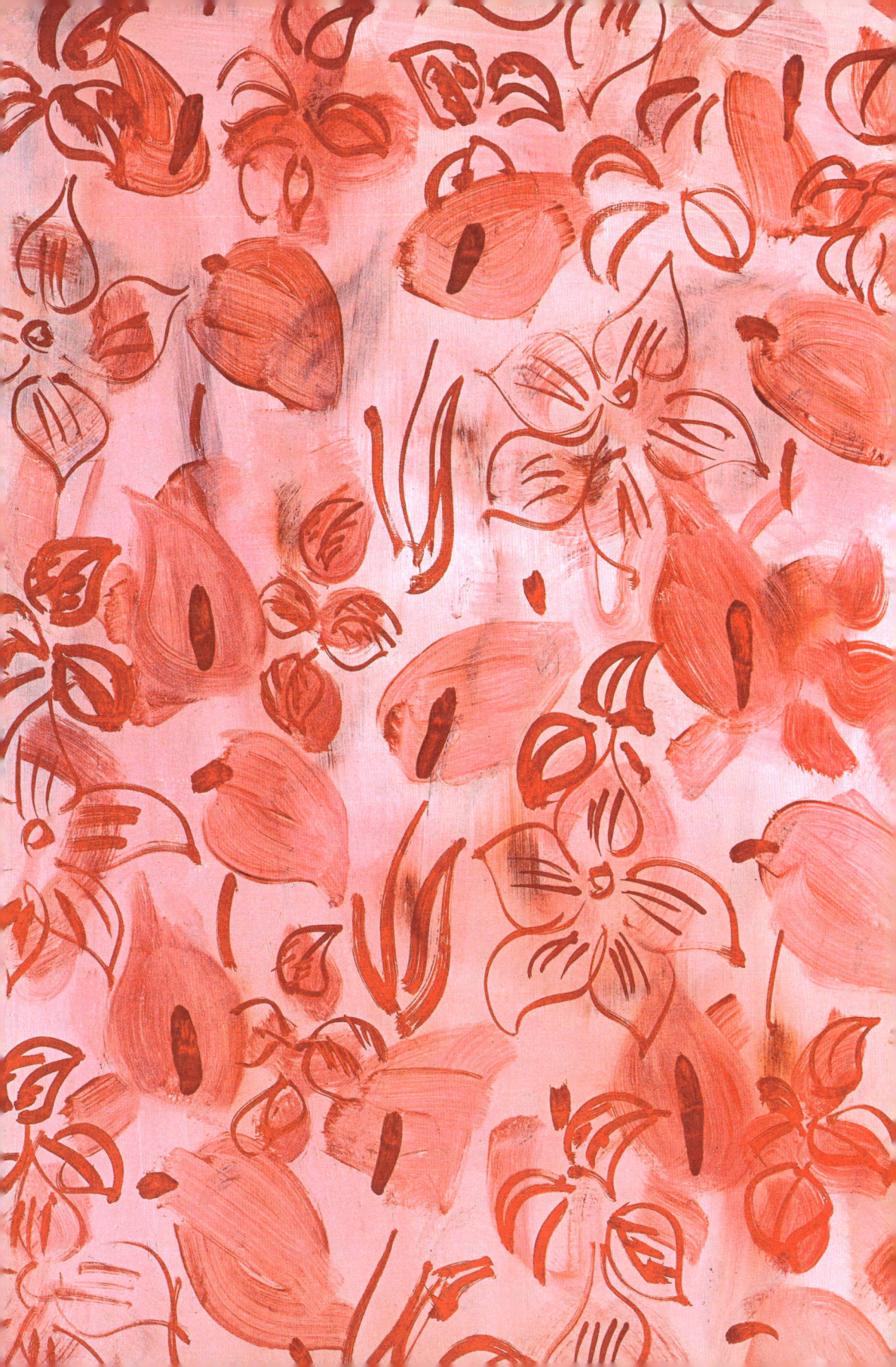

Surrounded Islands

1980-83

A bed of roses

The works of Christo and Jeanne-Claude are at once sculpture, architecture and art installations. Close to land Art, their practice developed out of a reflection on gigantism, a questioning of identity and our perception of space.

In Biscayne Bay on the Miami coast there are eleven islands which Christo and Jeanne-Claude decided to encircle with fuchsia-coloured polypropylene. To realise this installation, they had to obtain the necessary authorisations and respect the natural environment they were about to transform. They chose polypropylene because it has no effect on the flora and fauna in contact with it, and they also removed forty tons of rubbish from the islands which had become public dumping grounds.

When the project was completed, for two weeks the population could discover these islands metamorphosed by their floating pink skirts. Christo and Jeanne-Claude chose the colour pink because they wanted to create a striking contrast between the natural colours of the sea and vegetation and this vivid, artificial, synthetic colour powerfully emphasizing their human intervention. This pink also recalls Florida's South American identity, the candy colours of Miami Art Deco and also the pink flamingos inhabiting the coastline.

The couple redefined and reinterpreted the landscape to challenge our perception of it and recall its existence and beauty, but to also remind the local communitiy of its disastrous abuse of nature. And, paradoxically, by challenging our perception, this vivid, shocking, chemical pink also served as an ecological manifesto.

Surrounded Islands,
Christo and Jeanne-Claude
1980-83
Polypropylene
Ephemeral installation
Biscayne Bay, Miami, Florida

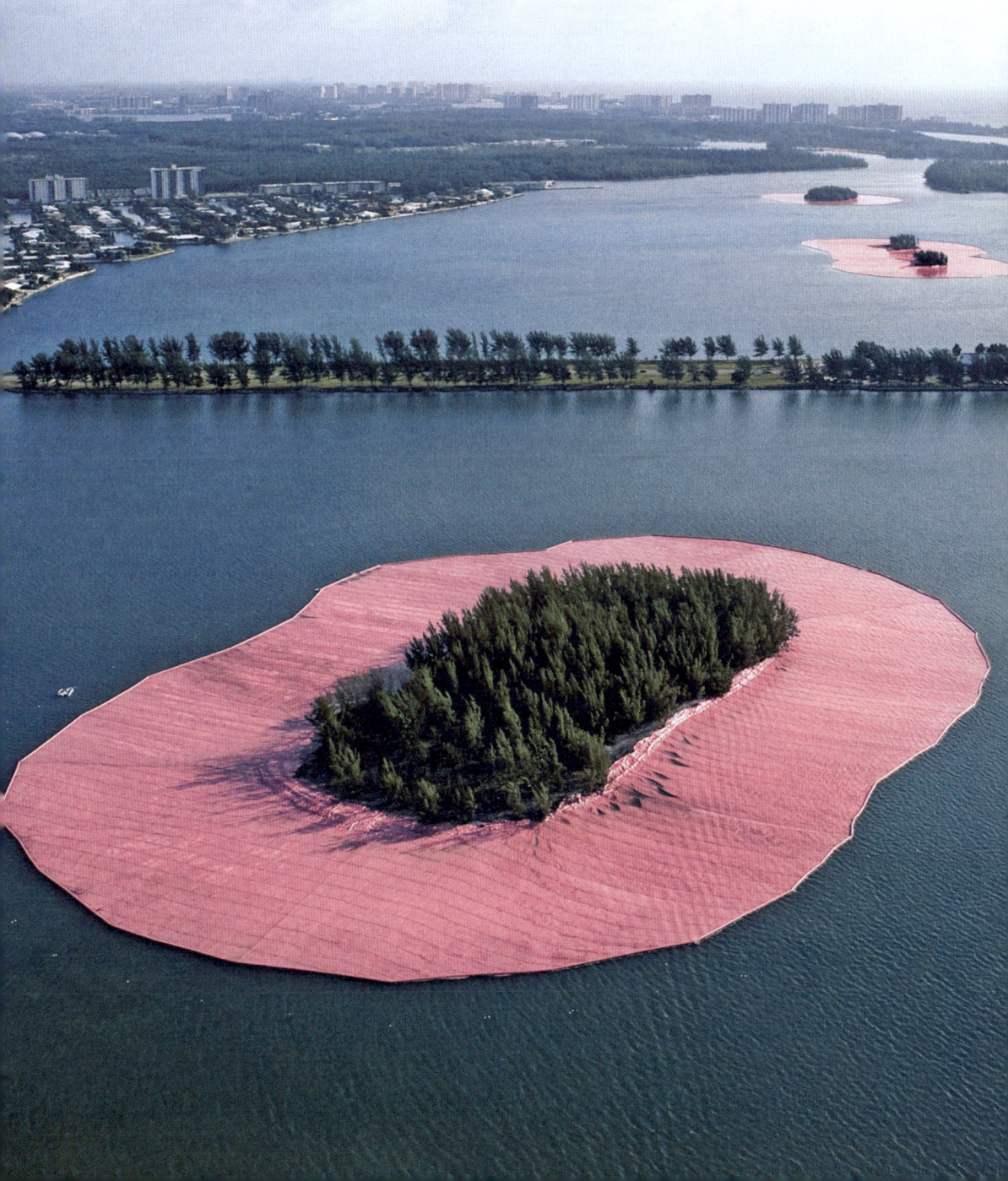

I want neither to freeze or perturb the places where I intervene. I'm simply trying to create moments of surprise and wonderment.

Christo and Jeanne-Claude

Be Calm

2005

TIMELINE
La vie
en rose

1949	The Blind Leading the Blind
Mamelles	1991
1995	Programme Guide
Pink Days and Blue Days	1997
2000	Temper Tantrum
Couple	2004
2010	Looking for the Mother

Be Calm,
Louise Bourgeois
2005
Drypoint on paper

An Appeal for Calm

In 1609 Louyse Bourgeois was the first midwife to write a book on obstetrics. So when the artist of the same name, Louise Bourgeois, was invited by the publishers Salon Verlag to contribute to its Ex Libris series in 2005, she naturally paid tribute to her namesake.

Since 2002 the German publisher Gerhard Theewen has invited artists to create new editions of books that had a major impact on their work. For Louise Bourgeois, it was *Recueil des secrets de Louyse Bourgeois, dite Boursier,* first published in 1635. Given Louise Bourgeois' interest in the mother-child relationship, this choice is hardly surprising, especially since both women share the same name. How could it have been otherwise?

Louise Bourgeois drew from early childhood, so well that she did preparatory drawings to help her parents in their work restoring tapestries. Later, drawing helped her calm her thoughts and anxieties and, as if by coincidence, the title of this work is *Be Calm.* A mantra, a message so simple but sometimes so difficult to put into practice, expressed in the simple form of an egg.

The three other lithographs in the book evoke pregnancy and childbirth. Was she seeking to allay the fears of a mother-to-be? Is this round, delicate pink egg an incarnation of her foetus?

There is another version of this drawing, in blue, as if Louise Bourgeois imagined two possible embryos, a girl in pink and a boy in blue. She is reassuringly, soothingly telling us to 'be calm', reminding us that there is a great adventure concealed in this egg. So we contemplatively, calmly lose ourselves in this oval full of promise, mystery and anxiety.

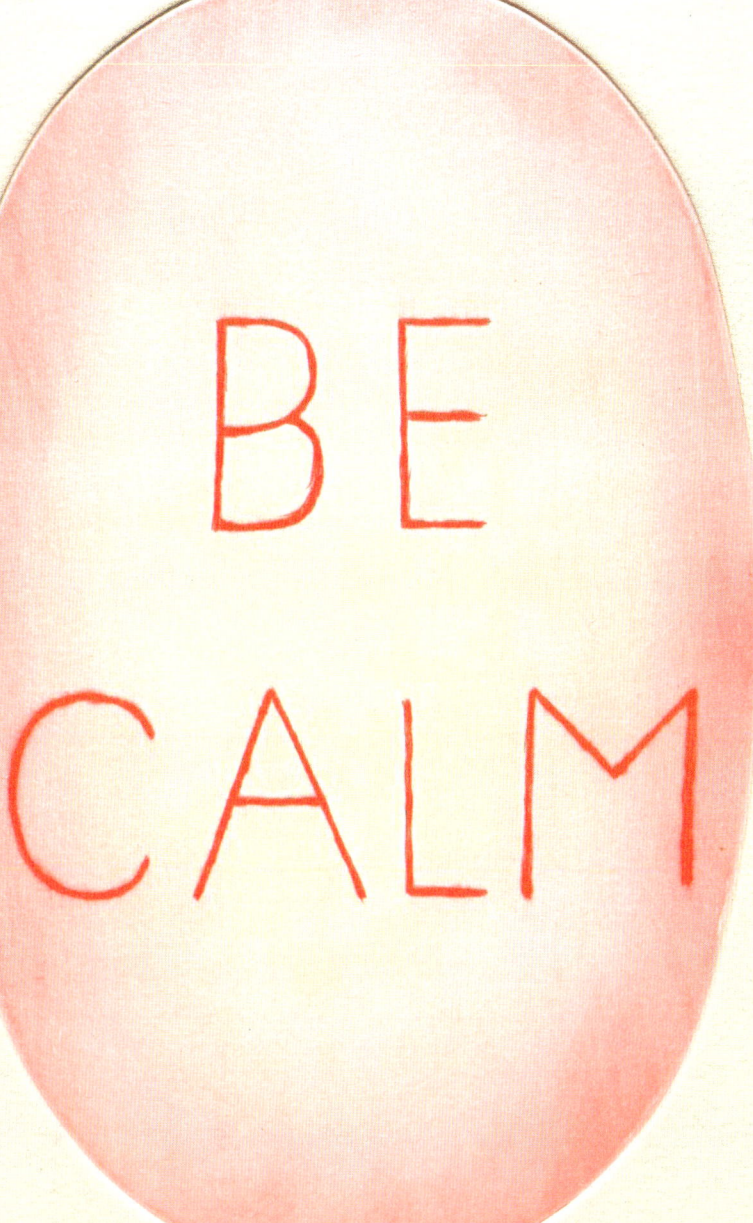

BE
CALM

Louise Bourgeois

AP 5/15

An Homage to Monopink 1960 A

2012

The First Time

In 1961 Yves Klein created an ex-voto composed of three blocks of pigments: gold (the Father), his IKB blue (the Son) and pink (the Holy Spirit). He was showing his devotion to Saint Rita, the patron saint of lost causes worshipped in his hometown of Nice. This was the first time he used pink in one of his works.

Misleading Appearances

In the 1990s Takashi Murakami founded the Superflat movement, denouncing the frivolity of Japanese consumer society in a style blending pop culture, tradition and vivid colours.

This composition belongs to one of his series on the flower motif, which he explored in numerous mediums. Our eye darts everywhere, trying not to lose itself in the profusion of multicoloured, childlike and rather kitschy flowers. Takashi Murakami's smiling, predominantly pink flowers are clearly referring here to both Japanese *manga* and the *kawai* 'cute' or 'adorable' style.

Murakami's work has many similarities with Andy Warhol's reflections on consumer society and art reproduction. He is reminding us of the trap of democratisation, in which everything is smoothed over, becomes the same and we all resemble one another.

There is something unsettling about this assemblage of flowers, too adorable to be sincere. Their forced smiles are threatening and their sheer number is frightening, invasive. With this supposedly charming imagery Murakami is showing us how we can so easily fall into the traps that society sets for us.

This work is a tribute to Yves Klein, who also created pink monochromes. But whereas in his use of pink the French artist was expressing his introspection on the soul and the flesh, the union of the spiritual and the material, Murakami is using it to denounce the baseness of a physical world preferring appearances to truth.

TIMELINE
Murakami Everywhere

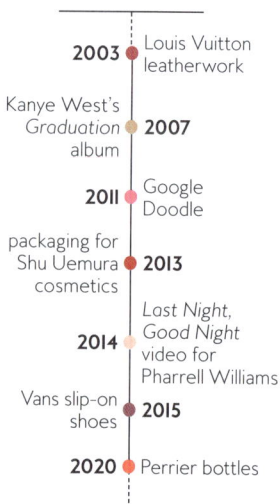

2003 Louis Vuitton leatherwork

Kanye West's *Graduation* album **2007**

2011 Google Doodle

packaging for Shu Uemura cosmetics **2013**

2014 *Last Night, Good Night* video for Pharrell Williams

Vans slip-on shoes **2015**

2020 Perrier bottles

An Homage to Monopink 1960 A,
Takashi Murakami
2012
Lithograph
Kunsthuis, Amsterdam

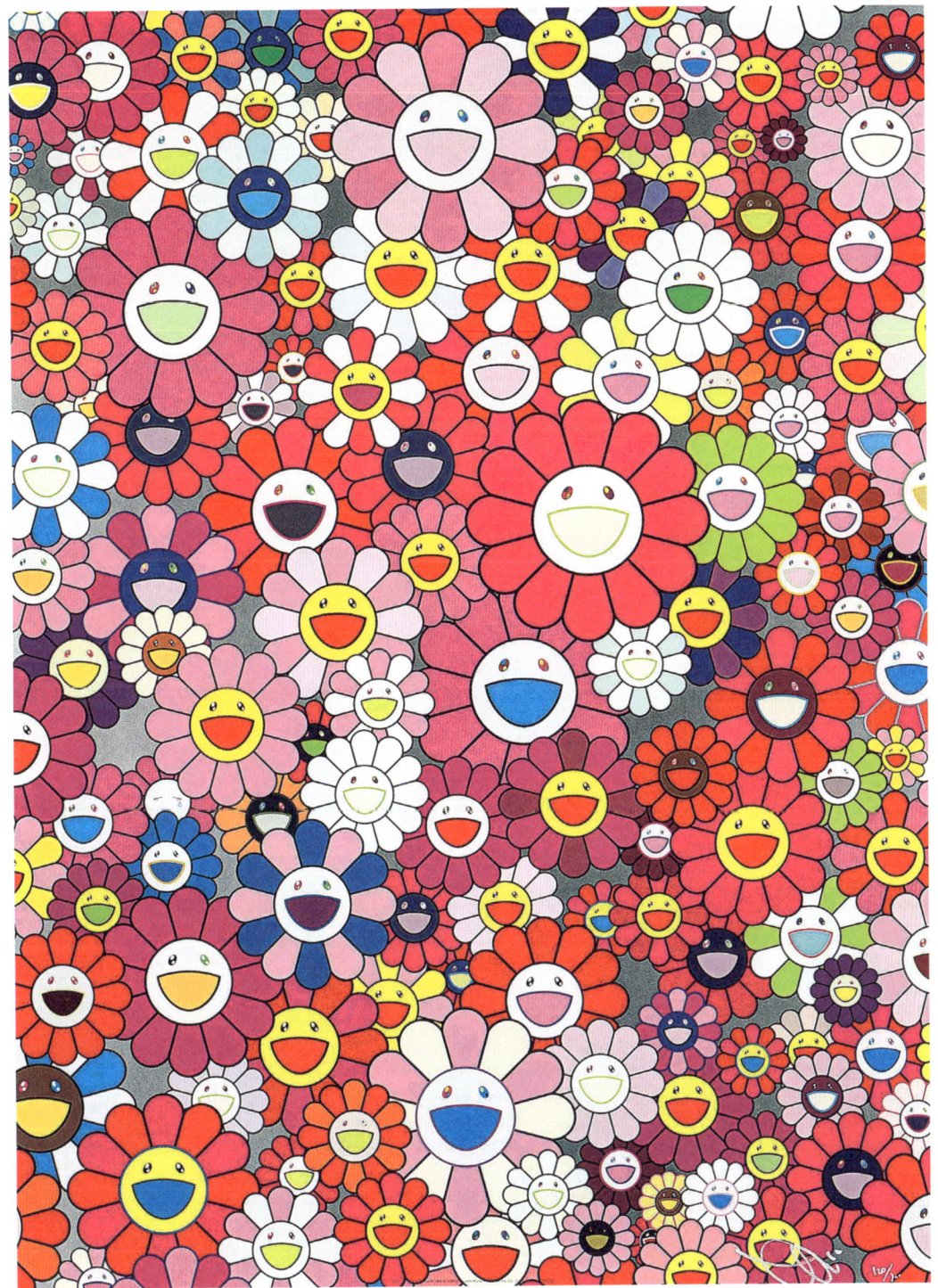

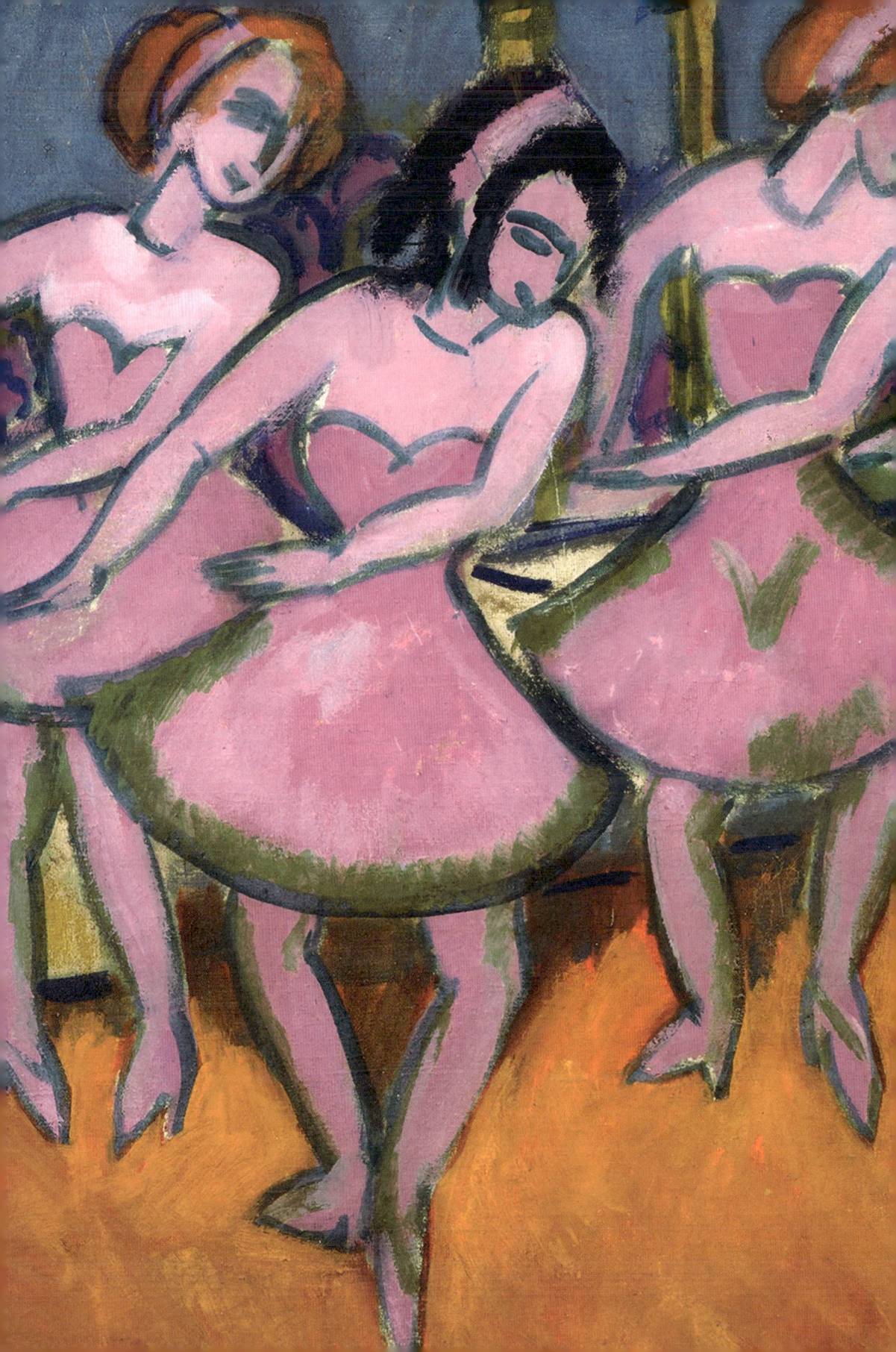

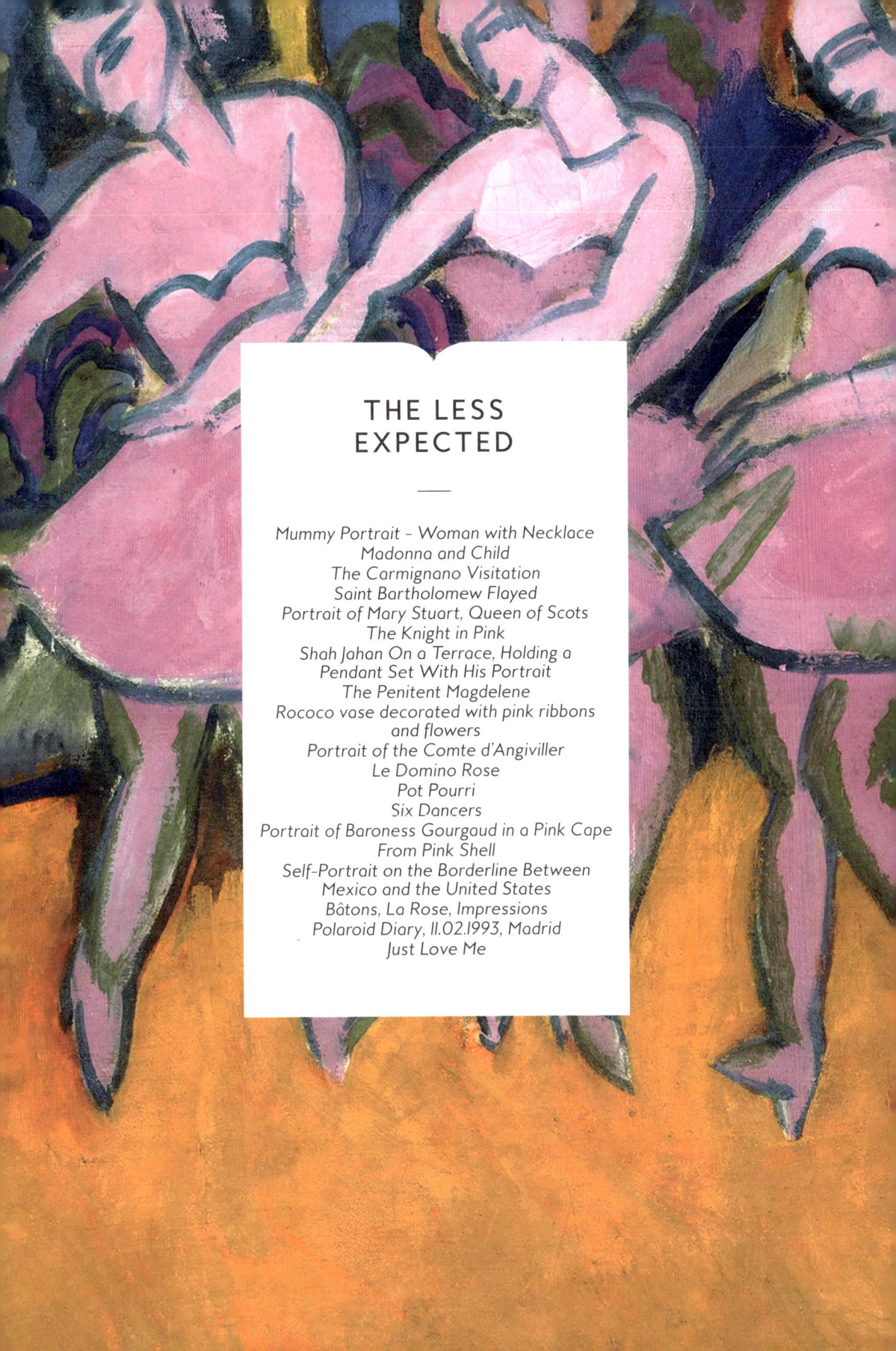

THE LESS EXPECTED

—

Mummy Portrait – Woman with Necklace
Madonna and Child
The Carmignano Visitation
Saint Bartholomew Flayed
Portrait of Mary Stuart, Queen of Scots
The Knight in Pink
Shah Jahan On a Terrace, Holding a
Pendant Set With His Portrait
The Penitent Magdelene
Rococo vase decorated with pink ribbons
and flowers
Portrait of the Comte d'Angiviller
Le Domino Rose
Pot Pourri
Six Dancers
Portrait of Baroness Gourgaud in a Pink Cape
From Pink Shell
Self-Portrait on the Borderline Between
Mexico and the United States
Bâtons, La Rose, Impressions
Polaroid Diary, 11.02.1993, Madrid
Just Love Me

Mummy Portrait – Woman with Necklace

A.D. 161–92

Mummy Portrait –
Woman with Necklace
A.D. 161–92
Encaustic on wood
Kunsthistorisches Museum, Vienna

In Death as in Life

In Roman Egypt from the first to the fourth century painted portraits were buried with the deceased, placed on the face of the mummified body. Many of them were found in the region of Fayum, hence the appellation 'Fayum portraits'.

These funerary images perpetuate the Egyptian belief in preserving the appearance of the deceased so that he or she can be recognised in afterlife. A combination of Roman portraiture and a pictorial style inherited from Greece, they are the earliest portraits painted on wood known in the ancient world. But more than their protective and ritual function, they strike us now with their commemorative role.

Although intended as commemorative portraits of the dead, they exude a moving sense of vitality. To achieve this, one has to imagine that they were painted during the individual's lifetime, because their frontality would have been unbecoming of the dead.

The artist portrayed this young woman in an oriental vein contradicting Greco-Roman canons, sensually bedecked in gold jewellery and a pink tunic. He accentuated her bust, outlined her lips and modelled her face with surprising voluptuousness when one considers the painting's purpose. There is definitely no solemnity or morbidity here. In afterlife one celebrates the life of the departed.

One therefore has to imagine the singular moment when the painter and the future deceased met. Did she ask him to change the colour of her garment or the shape of her eyes? Did she deliberately wear her favourite jewellery and arrange her hair in the latest fashion? For the artist, preserving a woman for eternity was a heavy responsibility.

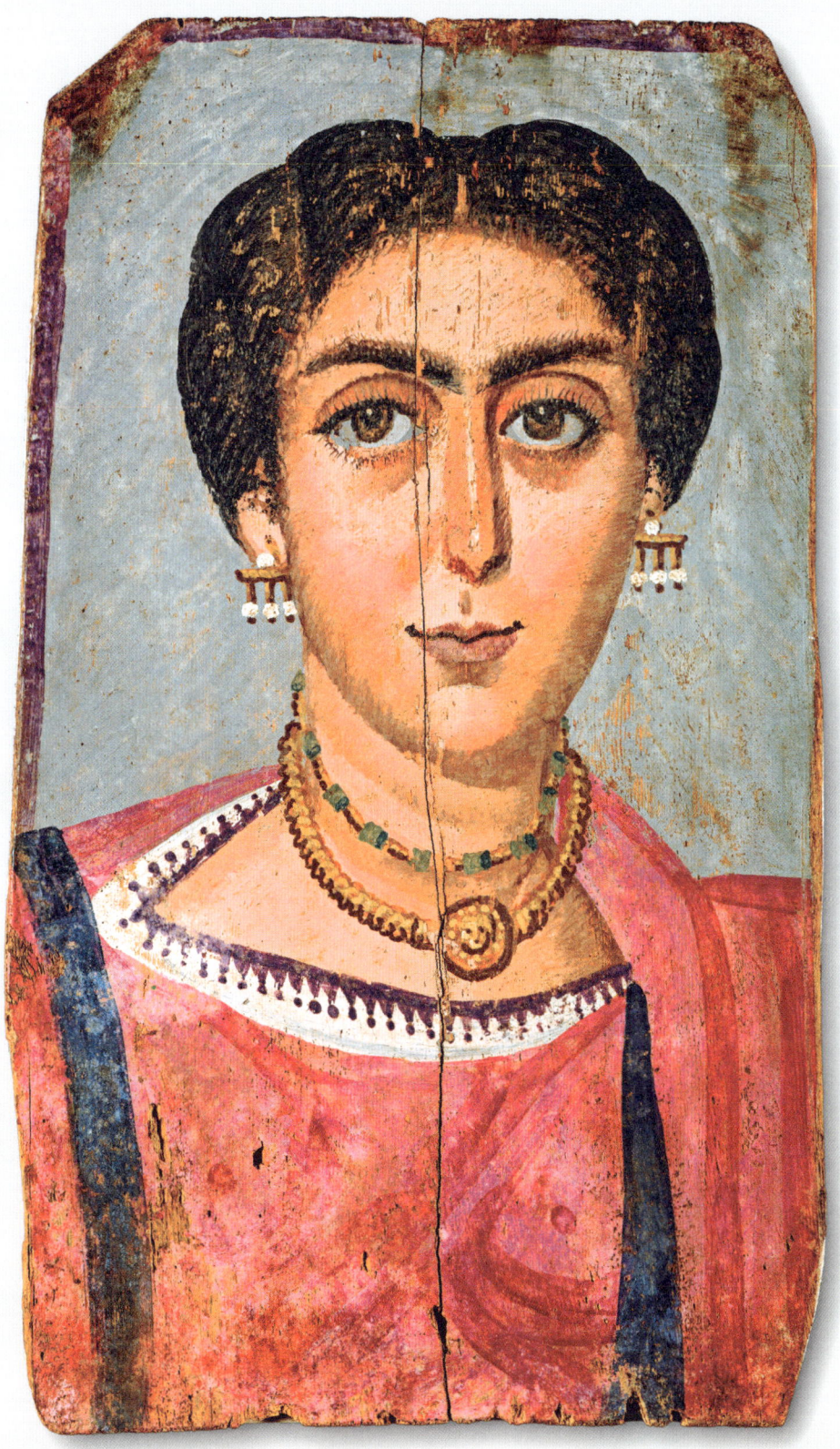

Madonna and Child

1480

Rosewood

During the Renaissance fabrics were dyed pink with Brazil wood, a variety of red wood from India or Brazil. Red, pink or violet tints were obtained depending on whether it was mixed with lime, ammonia or not. Dyers thought they were creating a light red colour not pink . . .

TIMELINE

Mother and daughter

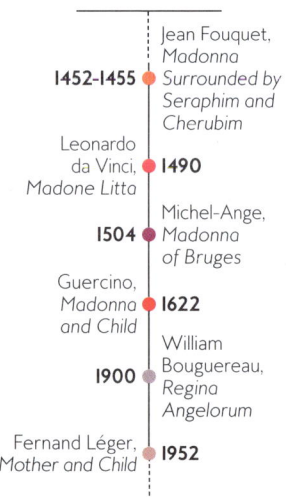

1452-1455	Jean Fouquet, *Madonna Surrounded by Seraphim and Cherubim*
Leonardo da Vinci, *Madone Litta*	**1490**
1504	Michel-Ange, *Madonna of Bruges*
Guercino, *Madonna and Child*	**1622**
1900	William Bouguereau, *Regina Angelorum*
Fernand Léger, *Mother and Child*	**1952**

Madonna and Child,
Carlo Crivelli
1480
Tempera and gold on wood
The Metropolitan Museum of Art,
New York

Enchanted Parenthesis

The Venetian Carlo Crivelli excelled in religious works painted with the finesse and precision of Flemish art. His *Madonna and Child* is full of symbols intended for our contemplation.

There is something unreal about this Virgin with perfect features, like a porcelain doll, delicate, graceful and therefore vulnerable. The subject, the happiness of Christ's mother and the fateful destiny of her son, was a perfect pretext for this ambivalent portrayal.
There is no smile on this sovereign doll's face. Carlo Crivelli had no intention of humanising her. He is glorifying her in all her majesty, a majesty heightened by her exquisite gold-embroidered robe and halo adorned with precious stones.

He gave the infant Jesus charming folds on his arms and legs to give him the appearance of a plump, well-fed baby. He is holding the little goldfinch like a child would a toy, but we are reminded of his divine status by his richly decorated halo. He is staring at the disproportionately large fly that has alighted next to him, not by chance. It represents evil, just as the oversized apples above embody sin.

To alert the viewer to the adversaries of Christianity, Crivelli also placed turbaned figures in the background, probably Turks and therefore infidels. And to re-establish equilibrium he painted a surprising cucumber by way of redemption, echoing the bird fondled by Christ.

Crivelli added a sentiment of grandeur and devotion in the Virgin's pink backdrop and the infant Jesus's pink cushion. This pink seems to be protecting them with its more prestigious tint of red, treated with gentleness to remind us that this child with such a great destiny awaiting him is still a baby in his mother's arms.

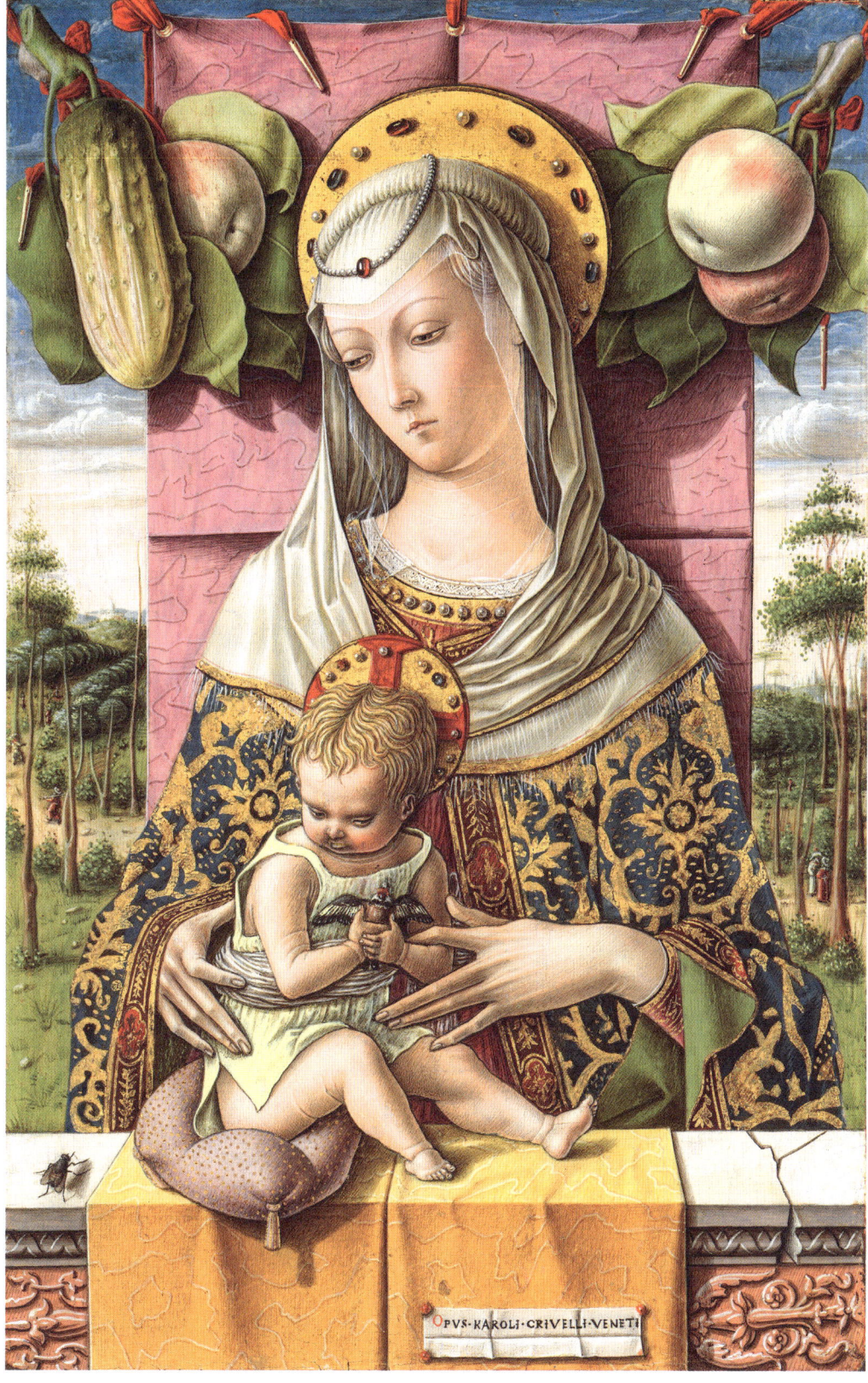

OPVS·KAROLI·CRIVELLI·VENETI

The Carmignano Visitation

1528-30

What Is the Visitation?

The Gospel of Saint Luke recounts the visit of Mary, pregnant with Jesus, to her cousin Elisabeth, herself pregnant with Saint John the Baptist. When the Virgin greets her cousin, she feels her child tremble and is filled with the Holy Spirit. The words spoken by Elisabeth are used in the Hail Mary prayer.

The Visit Filmed

In 1995, the artist Bill Viola created a thirteen-minute video, *The Greeting*, inspired by Pontormo's picture.

Doubles

In the late 1520s Pontormo, one of the principal Italian Mannerist artists, painted an altarpiece for the Pinadori family, destined for the church of Saint Michael and Saint Francis at Carmignano.

Pontormo preferred diverted perspectives, oversized figures and intense colours over the classicism and conventions of his contemporaries. His subjects here, the Virgin Mary and her cousin Elisabeth, have monumental presences as they meet in the streets of a city so geometricized and monochrome as to be almost abstract.

Mary and Elisabeth's embrace is echoed by the two women close behind them. Gazing straight at us in contrast to the two profiles in front of them, they seem to be returning our own gaze and inviting us to concentrate on the scene and its emotional intensity.

Some believe that these two women are servants, but could they be repetitions of Mary and Elisabeth? It is as if Pontormo wanted to show us what we cannot see in their embrace: their exchange of looks. Because he knew that it is those looks that say everything, did he choose to negate the eclipse of their profiles and involve us more directly in the scene?

Pontormo unified the four figures with vivid, contrasting yet complementary colours. Given the opposition between the Virgin Mary's blue tunic and the red garment of her double, one wonders whether the artist was showing us the two faces of Mary. In pink she is still a young woman in love, in blue she is the majestic woman whose child would have such an immense destiny.

The Carmignano Visitation,
Pontormo
1528–30
Oil on wood
Propositura dei Santi Michele e
Francesco, Carmignano

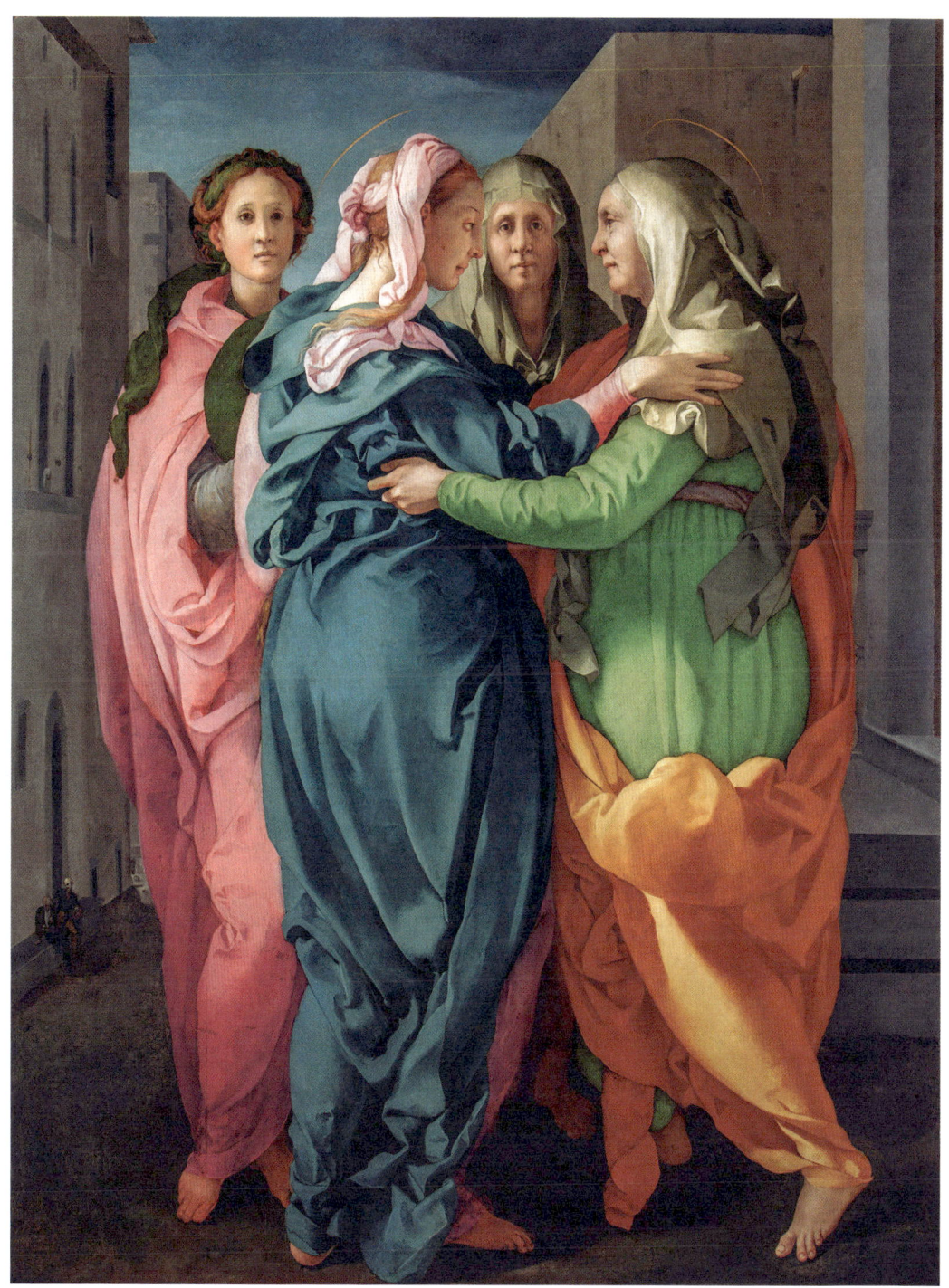

Saint Bartholomew Flayed

1556

TIMELINE

Anatomies and dissected corpses

1510-1511	Leonardo da Vinci, *Muscles of the shoulder, arm and neck*
Rembrandt, *The Anatomy Lesson of Doctor Nicolaes Tulp*	1632
1745	Jacques-Fabien Gautier d'Agoty, *The Anatomical Angel*
Honoré Fragonard, *Horseman of the Apocalypse*	1766-1771
1818-1819	Théodore Géricault, *Anatomical Pieces*
Francis Bacon, *Three Studies for a Crucifixion*	1962
2020	Lucile Boiron, *Mise en pieces*

Saint Bartholomew Flayed,
Bronzino
1556
Oil on panel
Galleria dell'Accademia Nazionale
di San Luca, Rome

The Salvation of the Body

In the mid-sixteenth century there emerged an artistic trend exalting serpentine lines, elongated figures and vivid colours. In his works with illusory, raw forms the Italian Bronzino became one of the major artists of the Mannerist style.

One can only describe this picture as raw. One could add disturbing, even violent, for a flayed body is difficult to look at. Yet frequently, especially during the Renaissance, artists preoccupied with scientific realism consulted anatomical treatises and even dissected corpses themselves. It is highly likely that Bronzino was inspired here by Andreas Vesalius's *De Humani Corporis Fabrica Libre Septem*, published in 1543.

The Mannerist artists wanted to go beyond the aesthetic canons, founded in Antiquity, of artists such as Michelangelo and Leonardo da Vinci. Strangely, this quest for a more organic representation expressed itself in exaggerated anatomies, as if to achieve more realism one had to transcend reality.

In this religious subject, Bronzino is depicting the apostle Bartholemew flayed alive. The musculature of his body is meticulously depicted and his skin and the knife used to flay him are shown on the floor at his feet. The detailed depiction of the flesh on the saint's neck and fingers, his taut tendons and pink muscles evoke the brutality of his ordeal. In contrast, he is draping himself with a pink sheet and a fuchsia-coloured drapery is hanging down over him, hues opposing yet complementing the shades of his tortured anatomy. Bronzino is recalling the prime role of art here: to reveal what we cannot see.

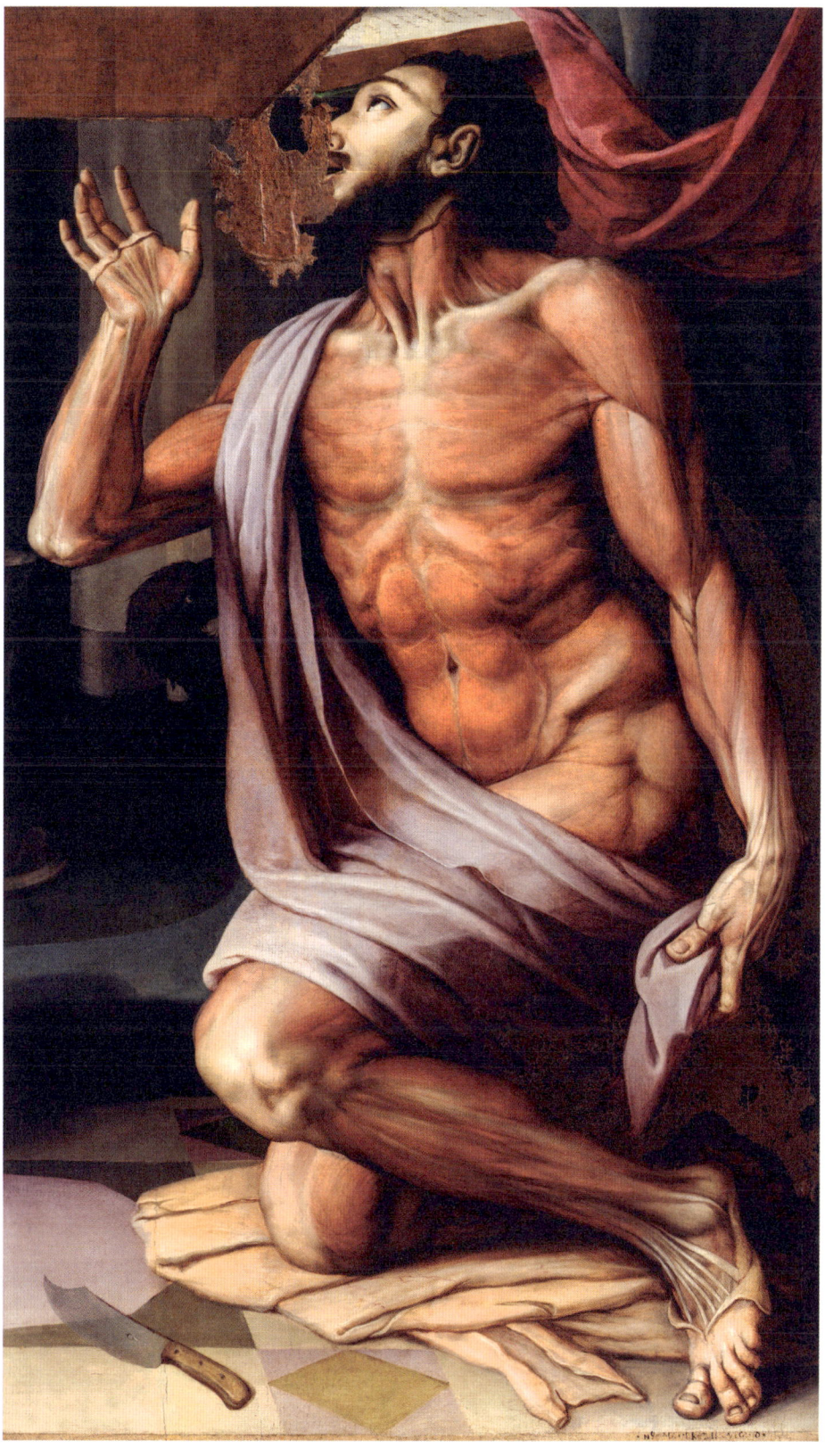

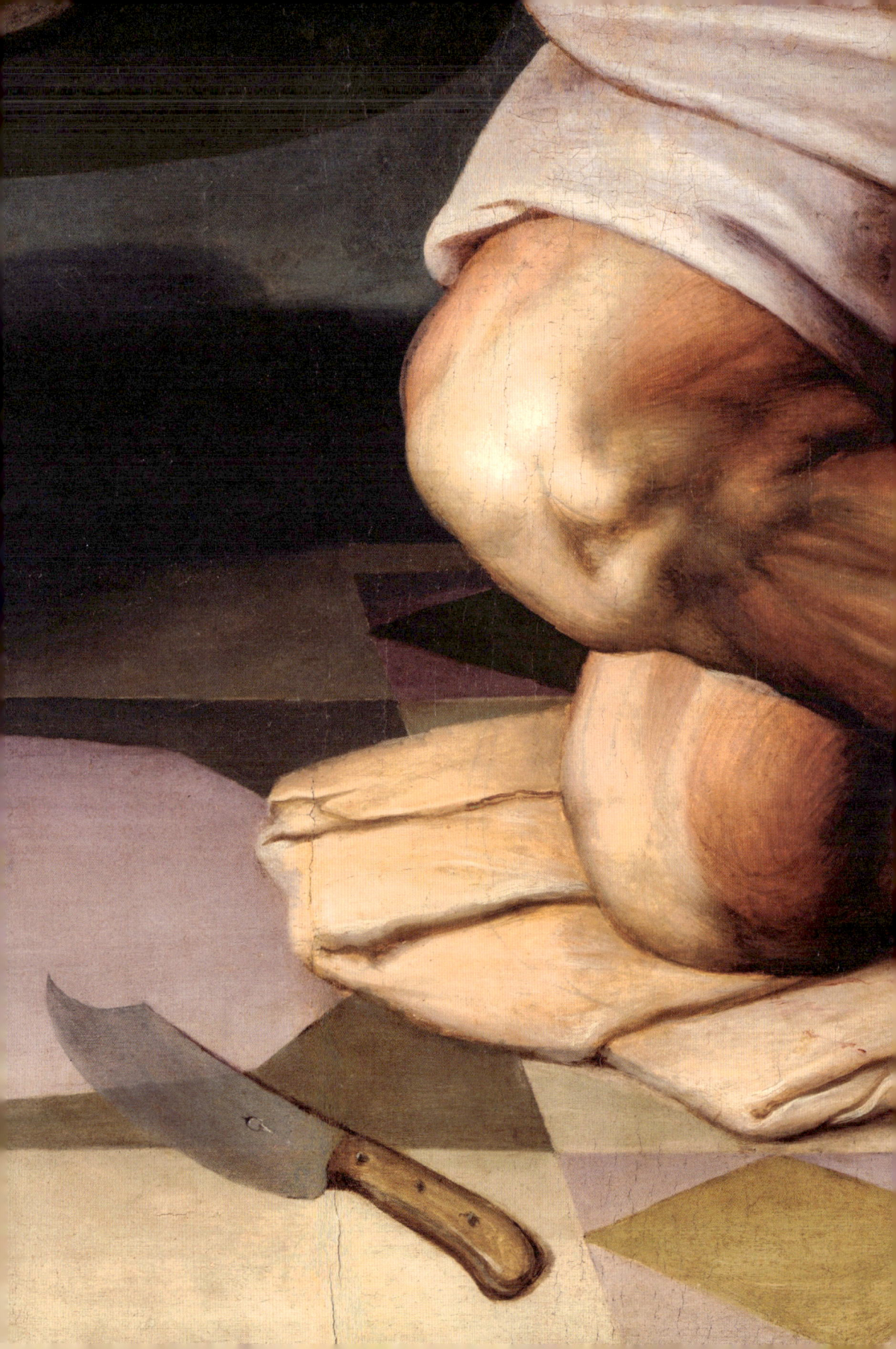

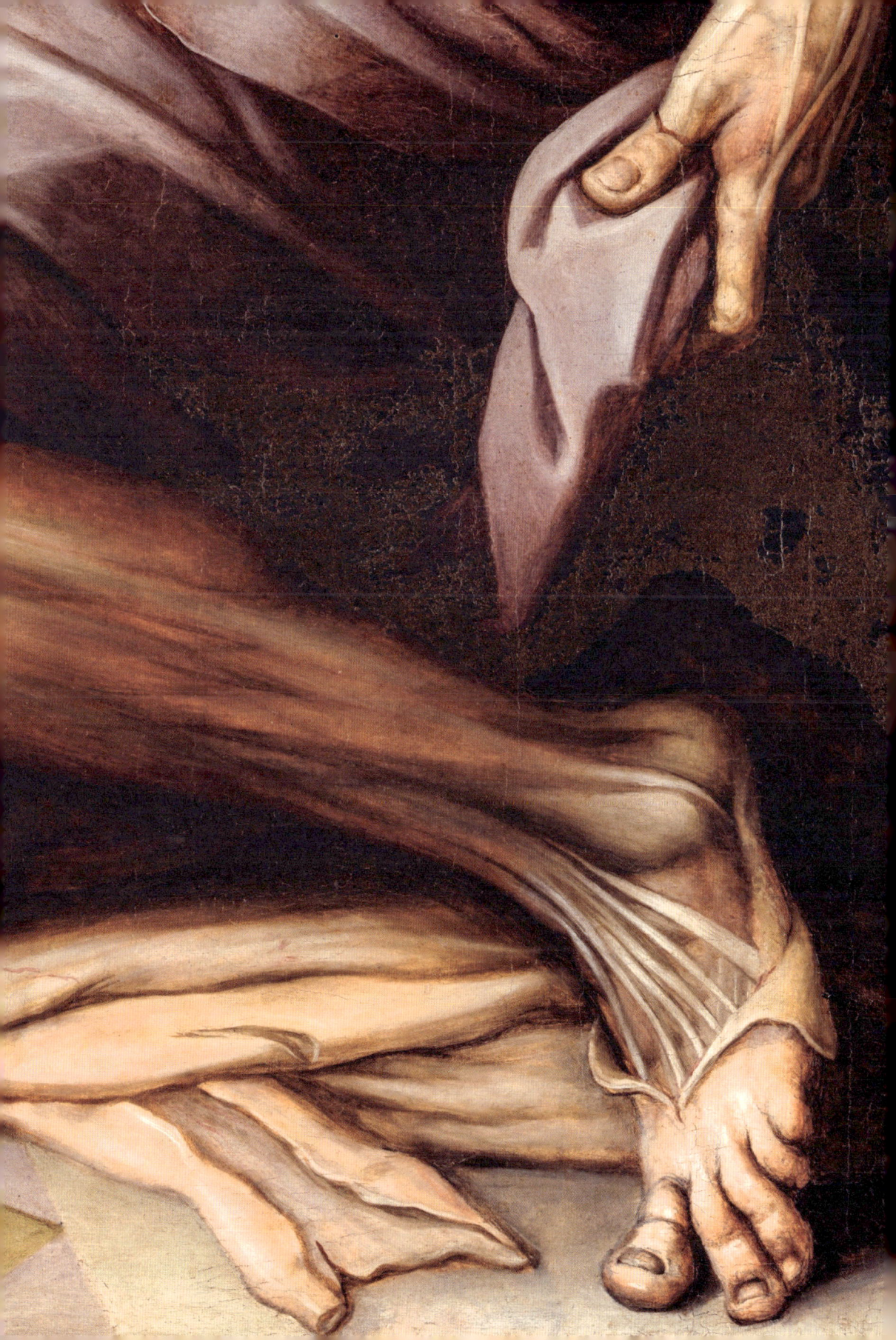

Portrait of Mary Stuart, Queen of Scots

1558

A Child Bride

François Clouet was a renowned painter and official royal portraitist. He portrayed the young Mary Stuart, future Queen of Scots, several times at the request of her mother Mary of Guise.

Mary Stuart was brought up in France, and this portrait shows her at the age of sixteen or seventeen, not long before her marriage to the future king, François II. Clouet shows her about to slip the ring on her right ring finger to signify this event. She is a very young woman whose future role will demand responsibility and nobility, who will soon have to prematurely become an adult.

Clouet portrayed Mary Stuart wearing a pink silk dress adorned with embroideries and pearls, then the height of fashion, its high collar and puffed sleeves accentuating her physique and rank. These vivid colours are symbols of power and the pearls adorning her hair and dress may well have been influenced by Italian fashion.

Clouet set his model against a neutral blue backdrop, enabling her to majestically occupy the picture space with her hands particularly emphasised. He is consecrating a young woman at the court of the Valois as an icon destined to be revered.

There is a picture, a copy of this miniature, which gives a dual role to this portrait: as a political statement glorifying the young woman's grandeur, but also as a more intimate image. Miniatures were usually destined for a person's close entourage or lovers. Was this young, hieratic, graceful Mary Stuart hoping to seduce her fiancé, to show him that she would make a worthy queen and loving wife?

Portrait of Mary Stuart, Queen of Scots,
François Clouet
ca. 1558
Watercolour on vellum
Royal Collection Trust, London

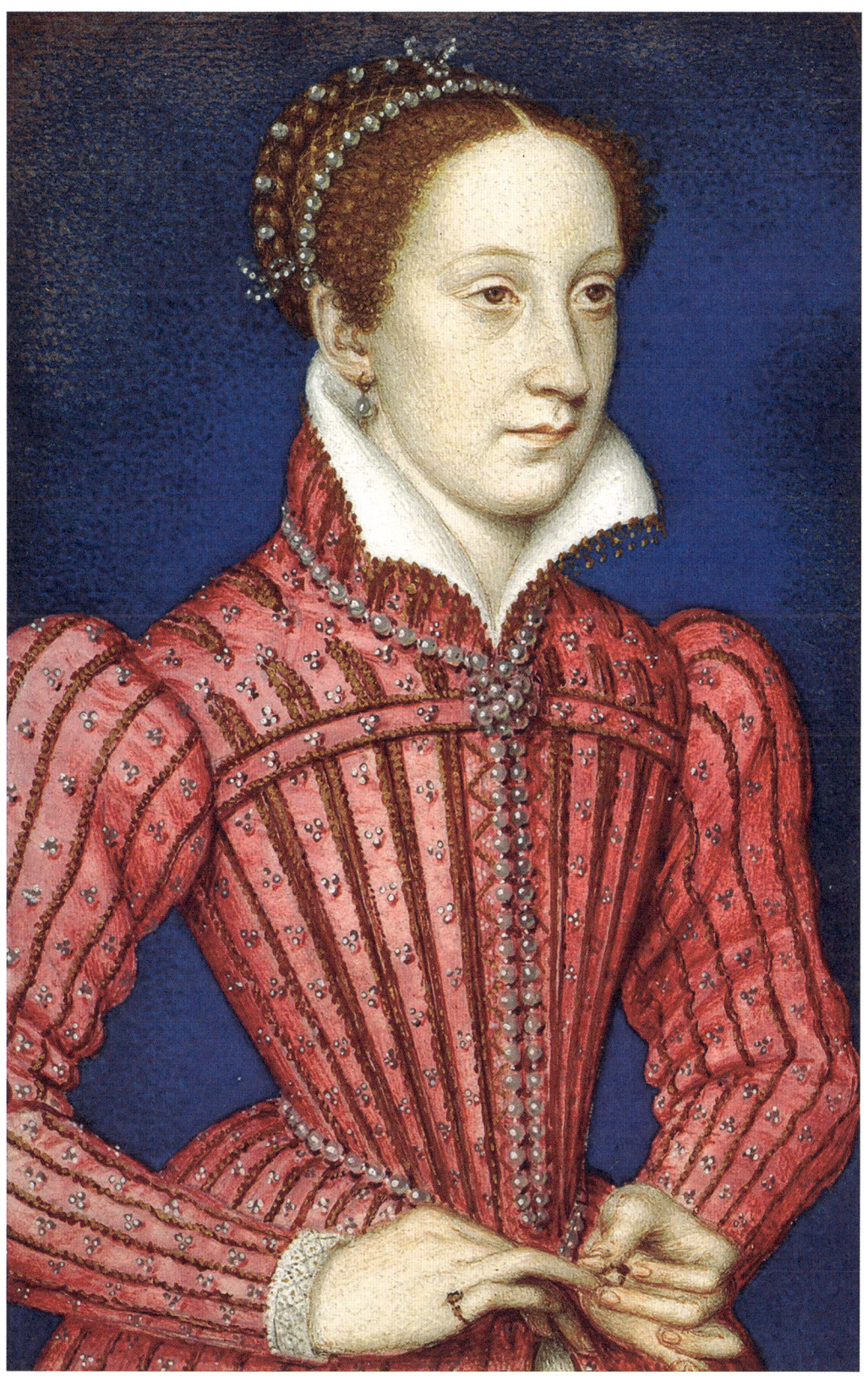

The Knight in Pink

1560

The Velvet Touch

Initially produced in the East, in India then in the Ottman Empire, silk velvet very soon became a sign of social status. The most renowned velvet manufactories were in Italy, in Venice, Florence, Milan and Genoa.

Coral Pink

Coral has been used in decoration since prehistoric times. It red-orange tint is due to the presence of carotene. The pinkish variety is the most sought after.

Rose-tinted

Giovanni Battista Moroni was a renowned portraitist appreciated by Bergamo's aristocracy. He incorporated psychology and narration into his works to convey the interior and social worlds of his subjects.

He filled this full-length portrait with allusions to the life of this young gentleman, looking sideways at us with pride and dignity yet standing in front of a partially ruined architectural background. The statue lying broken on the ground also suggests the passage of time.

The bas-relief at the bottom on the right depicts a biblical scene: the prophet Elijah, taken away by a chariot of fire, leaving his mantle to his disciple Elisha. Both a fall and a transmission. Is this man seeking to show his wish to establish himself as an embodiment of modernity, as the epitome of a new generation establishing itself on the ruins of a bygone world?

His dignified pose is heightened by his coral pink attire ornately embroidered with silver thread. He is dressed in the latest, Spanish-influenced fashion: a closely fitting doublet with matching bouffant breeches and stockings. His virility is accentuated by the volumes below his waist, his upright torso and slim legs.

Moroni's decision to dress his knight in pink is no coincidence; the model's family emblem was a coral branch. The painter symbolised this with the vivid pink also present on the man's cheeks. A young man driven by the passion of youth and his nobility.

The Knight in Pink,
Giovanni Battista Moroni
1560
Oil on canvas
Fondazione Museo di Palazzo
Moroni, Bergamo

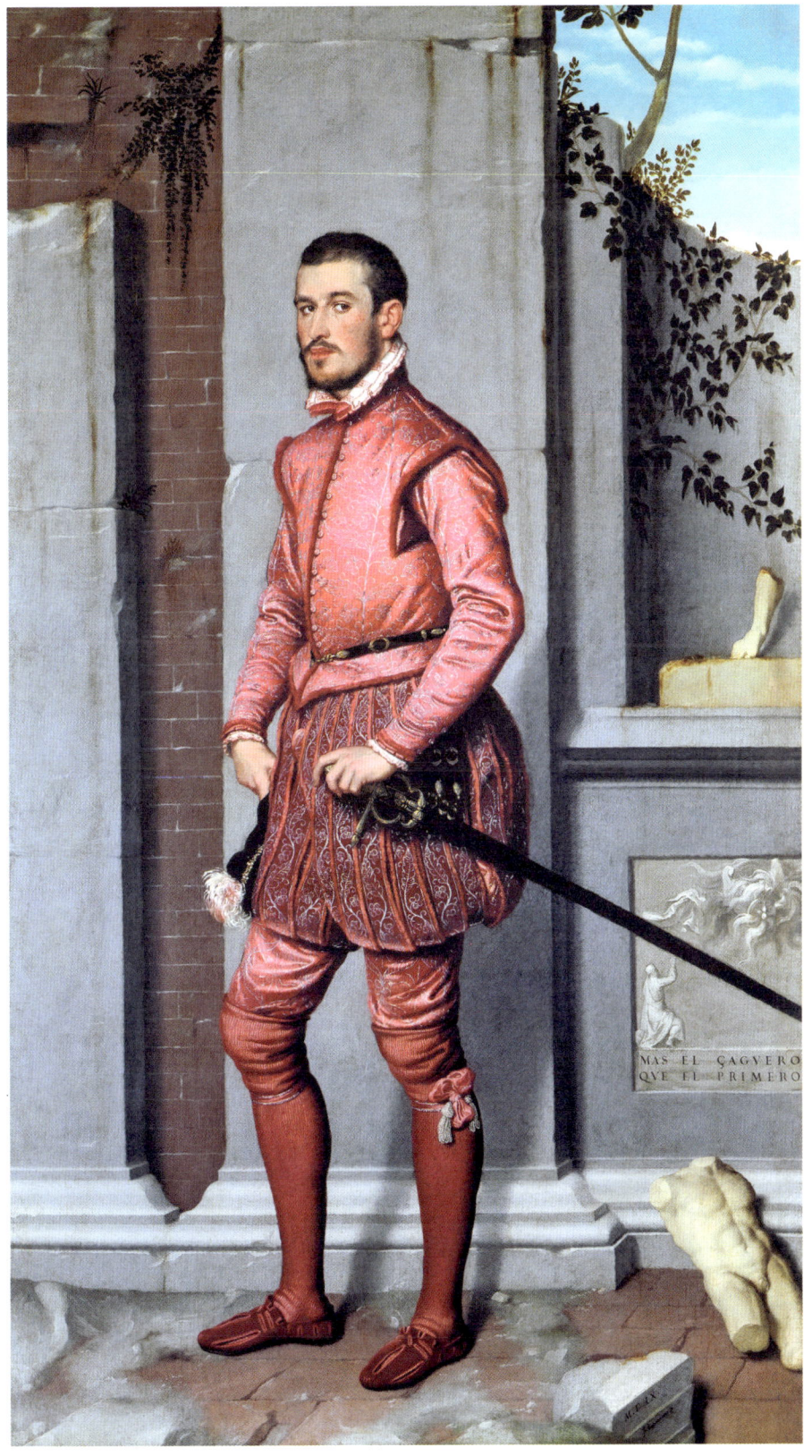

MAS EL ÇAGVERO
QVE EL PRIMERO

Shah Jahan On a Terrace, Holding a Pendant Set With His Portrait

1627/28

A Sacred Union

The Mughal Empire reached its peak in the sixteenth and seventeenth centuries, notably during the reign of Emperor Shah Jahan, whose name could be translated as 'king of the world'. Despite its small size (only 20 centimetres high) this portrait irradiates his splendour.

The emperor is portrayed framed with gold and a Turkish poem. Although painted in the recognisable style of Persian miniatures, the image is full of heterogenous influences. The cherubs and halo are inspired by European religious iconography and there are also references to Hinduism and Islam. The artist, Chitarman, was a Hindu, but the man who commissioned the work was a Muslim – an expression of the peace and tolerance then reigning in the Empire.

Shah Jahan is portrayed like a religious icon, encircled by coloured haloes. Hieratic, standing on a platform, he embodies stability and power. His glory expresses itself in the arts of his empire emphasised here: a floral carpet, the marble pedestal, the precious metalwork, jewellery, fabrics, featherwork and architecture.

Wearing the *sahra*, the pearl, ruby and emerald necklace usually worn by Muslim husbands, the emperor is narcissistically admiring a pendant depicting himself. His pink, floral-patterned tunic with an orange and gold sash is called the *jama*. He has knotted it on the right in the Muslim tradition, whereas a Hindu would have knotted it on the left. He is also wearing a violet turban decorated with peacock feathers, his attribute.

In Indian tradition, pink is associated with marriage. Shah Jahan is therefore exhibiting two references to union. The portrait he is looking at is perhaps a mark of this alliance. An emperor devoted to himself, to his power.

From Father to Son

The Shah Jahan album comprises some fifty illustrated and calligraphed folios. Emperor Jahangir commissioned its creation and his son Shah Jahen completed it in 1820

Self-adoration

It was Shah Jahan who built the Taj Mahal in memory of his wife. More a symbol of power than an expression of love, this white marble mausoleum is above all an example of the megalomania of an emperor who considered himself a divine presence.

Shah Jahan On a Terrace, Holding a Pendant Set With His Portrait
Chitarman
1627/28
Ink, watercolour and gold on paper
The Metropolitan Museum of Art, New York

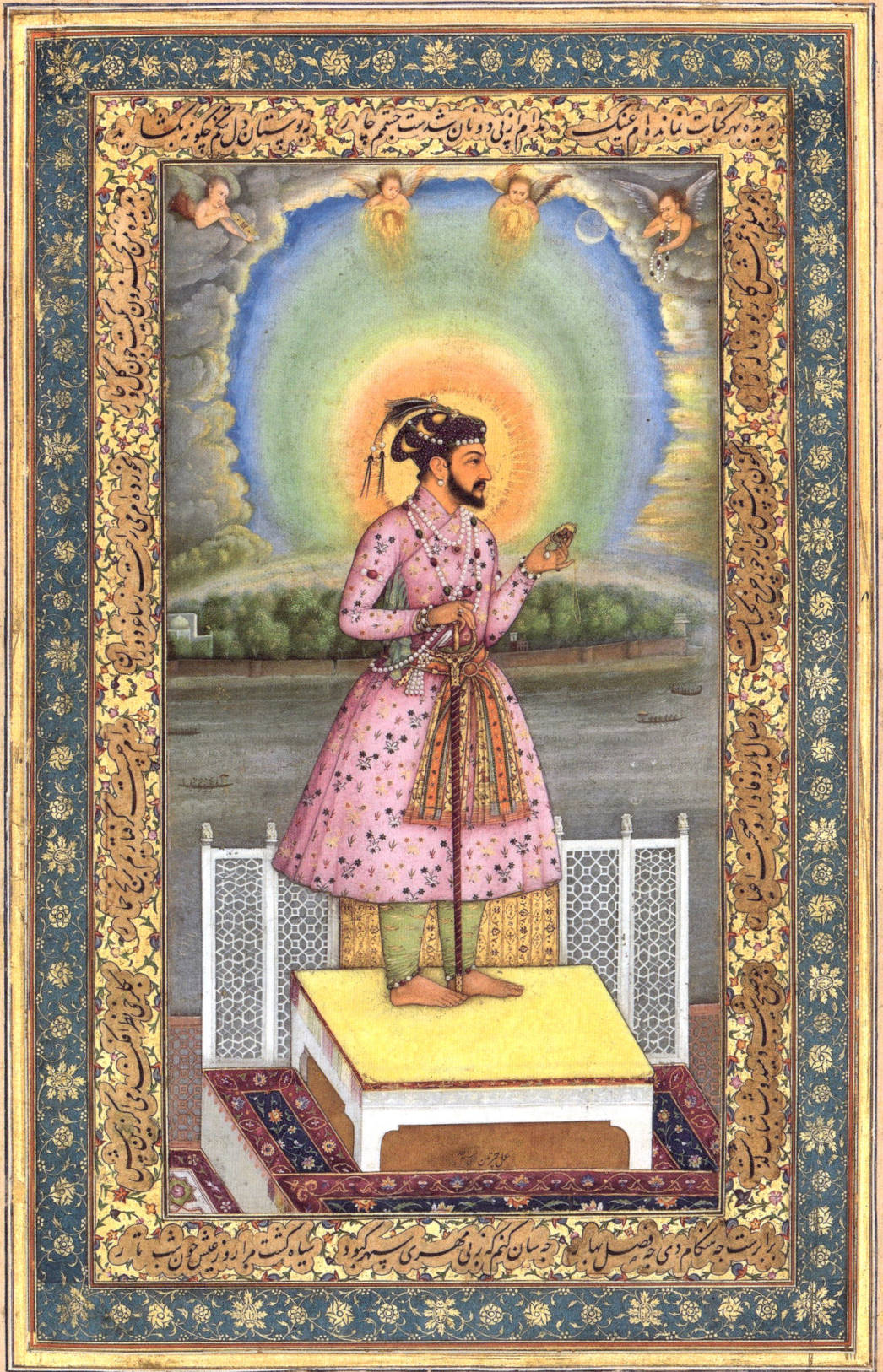

The Penitent Magdalene

1635

Pardon

Mary Magdelene

When she met Christ, shedding tears of repentance she poured perfume on his feet then dried them with her hair. Pardoned and delivered from her demons, she appears regularly in the New Testament. It was she whom Christ asked to announce his resurrection to the apostles. Tradition has it that she spent the last thirty years of her life in the Massif de la Sainte-Baume in Provence.

Symbolic Attributes

Skull: mortality
Ivy: eternal life, fidelity, resurrection
Jar: the perfume with which Mary Magdeleine washed Christ's feet

There is an air of ambiguity in this picture by Guido Reni. Although motivated by a quasi-Mannerist aesthetic and aspiring to the classical ideal, he was also influenced by the melancholic, obscure atmospheres of Caravaggio.

But unlike Caravaggio, in his portrayal of Mary Magdelene Reni emphasised light, even if his muted, nuanced treatment suggests that he wanted to convey her ambivalence. Mary Magdeleine is one of the prime subjects in Christian iconography because she symbolises penitence whilst enabling artists to depict a sensual, carnal female presence.

Her impure past permitted her portrayal as such, whereas her repentance renders her honourable in the eyes of the Church. Although supposedly indecent, she has milky skin heightened with pink nuances and golden hair. The faith inspired by her meeting with Christ is embodied by her heavenward gaze, yet she is meditating on the meaning of life in front of a skull surmounted by a cross.

Accentuating the gentleness of the image with soothing tones, Guido Reni fills this moment of religious ecstasy with an aura of calm strength, as if Mary Magdelene's newfound spirituality is infused with a serenity of which she is already aware. This picture exudes a clarity referring as much to divine light as Mary Magdelene's inner light. Her hand is pressed to her chest in a moment of revelation but also in a gesture of humility before the grandeur overcoming her. Is she is also asking for forgiveness? Guido Reni has already forgiven her.

The Penitent Magdalene,
Guido Reni
1635
Oil on canvas
The Walters Art Museum,
Baltimore

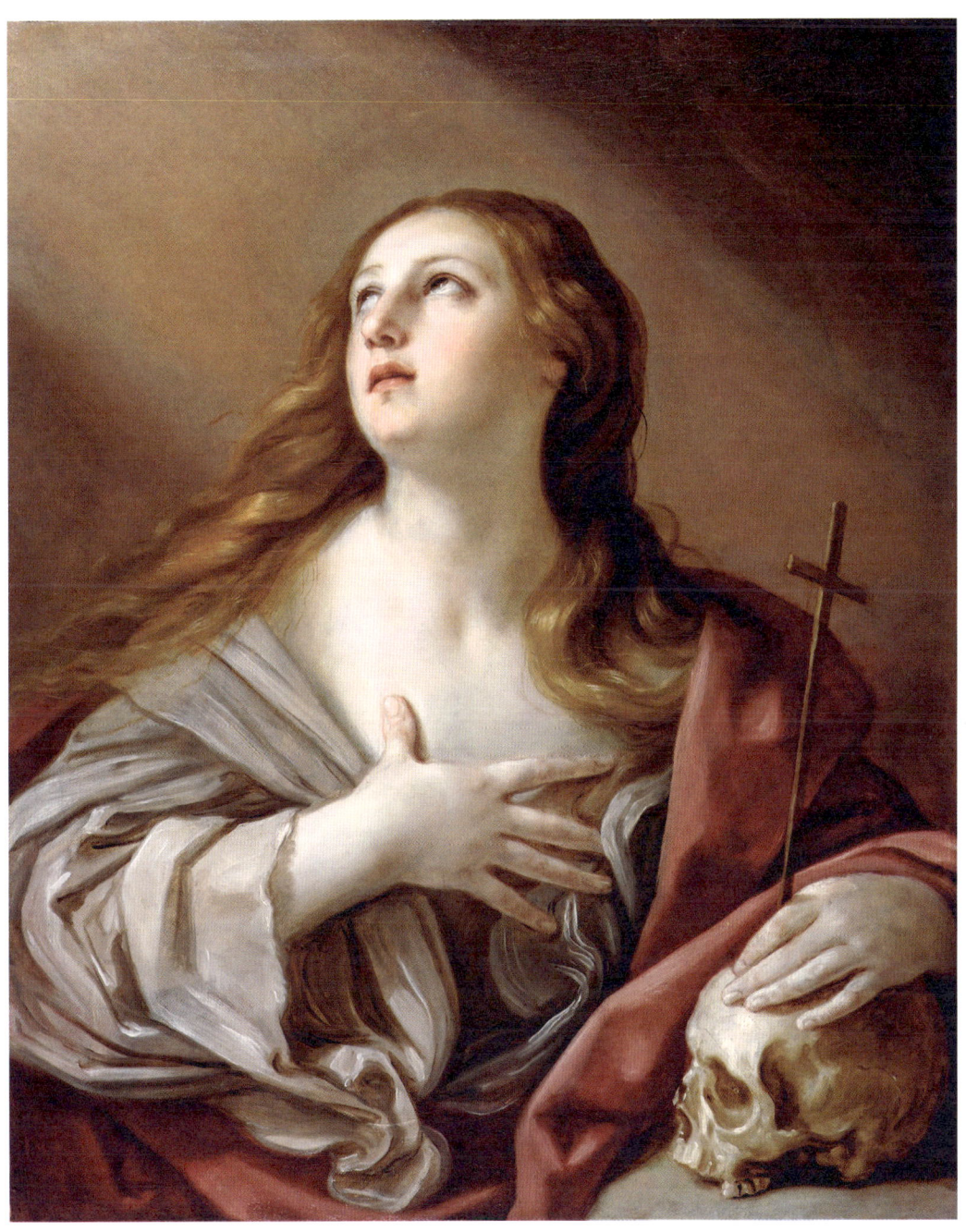

Rococo vase decorated with pink ribbons and flowers

1757/58

Soft-paste Porcelain

The Manufacture de Sèvres, initially established in Vincennes in 1740, produced soft-paste porcelain made from clay and glass frit. In the early 1770s it began producing hard-paste porcelain after the discovery of kaolin deposits in France.

Coloured Glazes

From 1749 to 1764 the manufactory excelled in its coloured glazes. The biscuit and its glaze were fired in two different kilns at a low temperature, leaving white areas for the painted decoration. 'Pompadour pink' was a mixture of a violet pigment, Cassius purple, and colloidal gold.

Rococo vase decorated with pink ribbons and flowers,
Manufacture de Sèvres
1757/58
Porcelain
Château de Versailles

Made in France

In 1757 the Manufacture de Sèvres perfected a colour described as 'a very fresh and pleasant pink' and baptised 'rose Pompadour' because this tint was so associated with the Madame de Pompadour. The manufactory produced objects in this pink for the first time in 1758. Louis XV acquired this vase.

Pastel tints were fashionable in the middle of the century as the Rococo style was giving way to Neoclassicism. Pink became increasingly prevalent in garments, decoration and artworks. Porcelain was no exception, especially as Madame de Pompadour popularised the colour at court in Versailles but also thanks to the popularity and influence of Sèvres porcelain.

The porcelain painter Philippe Xhrouet and the chemist Jean Hellot created this joyous, fanciful lilac-tinted pink. Here the pink ribbons combine with the graceful floral motifs while the vase's voluptuous form echoes its twirling decorative patterns. Pink and porcelain were the privilege of the aristocracy, to which gold was added as a mark of abundance.

This pink porcelain vase is a perfect illustration of the French craftsmanship and triumphant, luxurious style that had been transformed into a political weapon by Louis XIV. It is also a late example of the technique of colouring soft-paste porcelain that was the pride of the Manufacture de Sèvres.

Each year the manufactory's latest creations were exhibited in the royal apartments at Versailles, where those at court well knew that to remain in favour one had to offer a porcelain piece to the nation.

Who has visited Sèvres?
Who knows what goes on in that large, silent building,
seemingly asleep on the banks of the Seine?

Guy de Maupassant

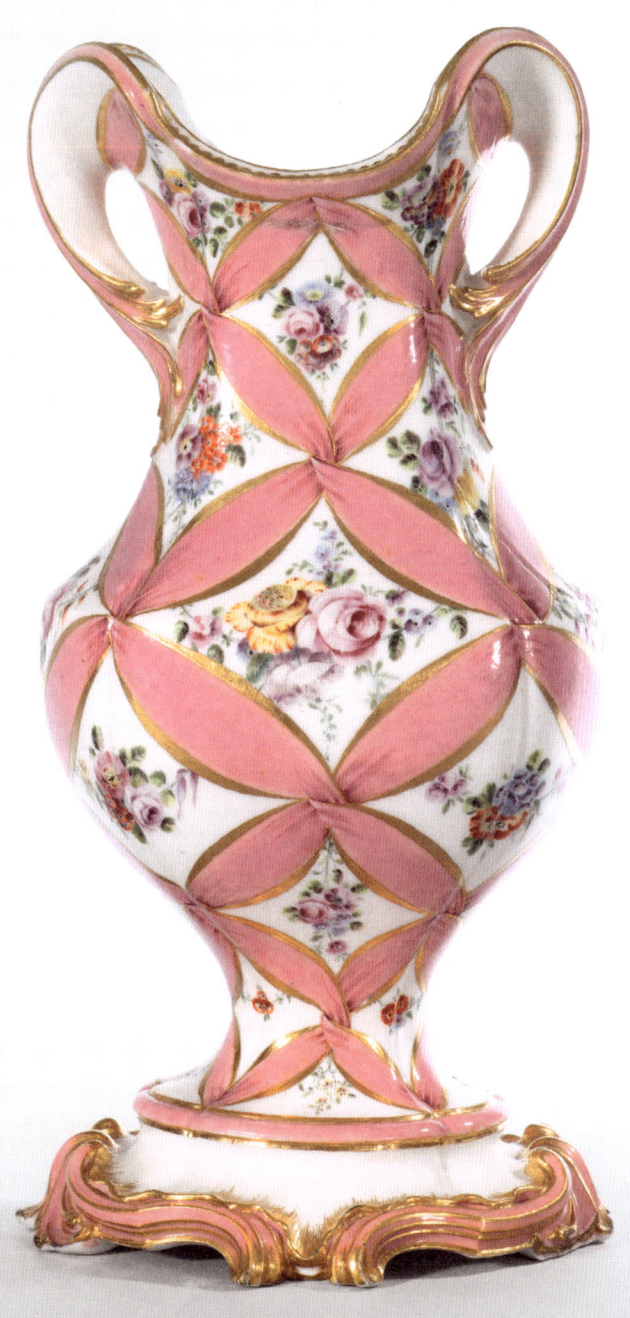

Portrait of the Comte d'Angiviller

ca. 1778

Portrait of the Comte d'Angiviller,
Joseph-Siffred Duplessis
ca. 1778
Oil on canvas
Château de Versailles

Elegance Personified

In 1774 The Comte d'Angiviller was appointed Director General of the King's Buildings, Arts, Gardens and Manufactories. In this role he promoted an antique-influenced style in the arts and architecture.

Neoclassicism became the norm in all creative and aesthetic disciplines, even in fashion. As the eighteenth century neared its end and the Revolution approached, there reigned a will to simplify aristocratic dress and a rejection of the ostentation of the baroque and the frills of rococo for more sober forms and unified motifs.

For this official portrait Joseph-Siffred Duplessis portrayed his subject in the splendour of his status. On the document unfurled before him we read 'Galerie du Louvre', because the king's director of buildings was considering the installation of the royal collection in the palace. The Comte d'Angiviller was an ambitious man who instigated numerous cultural initiatives, the acquisition of works and the transformation of some of Paris's districts.

The painter is emphasising the dignity of his model, dressed in the French style, symbol of the taste and excellence of his country. This style, initially promoted by Louis XIV, became the uniform of the aristocracy in the eighteenth century. D'Angiviller is dressed here in a resplendent lilac-pink silk outfit complemented by a cream waistcoat with delicate floral embroidery. There is nothing ostentatious about his pose or the décor, but we are impressed by the vivid colour of his attire.

Most of the known portraits of d'Angiviller show him dressed in pink or violet, in lighter shades of the royal purple red. Still a colour of great authority but a shade below royal, as if to avoid any hint of lèse-majesté.

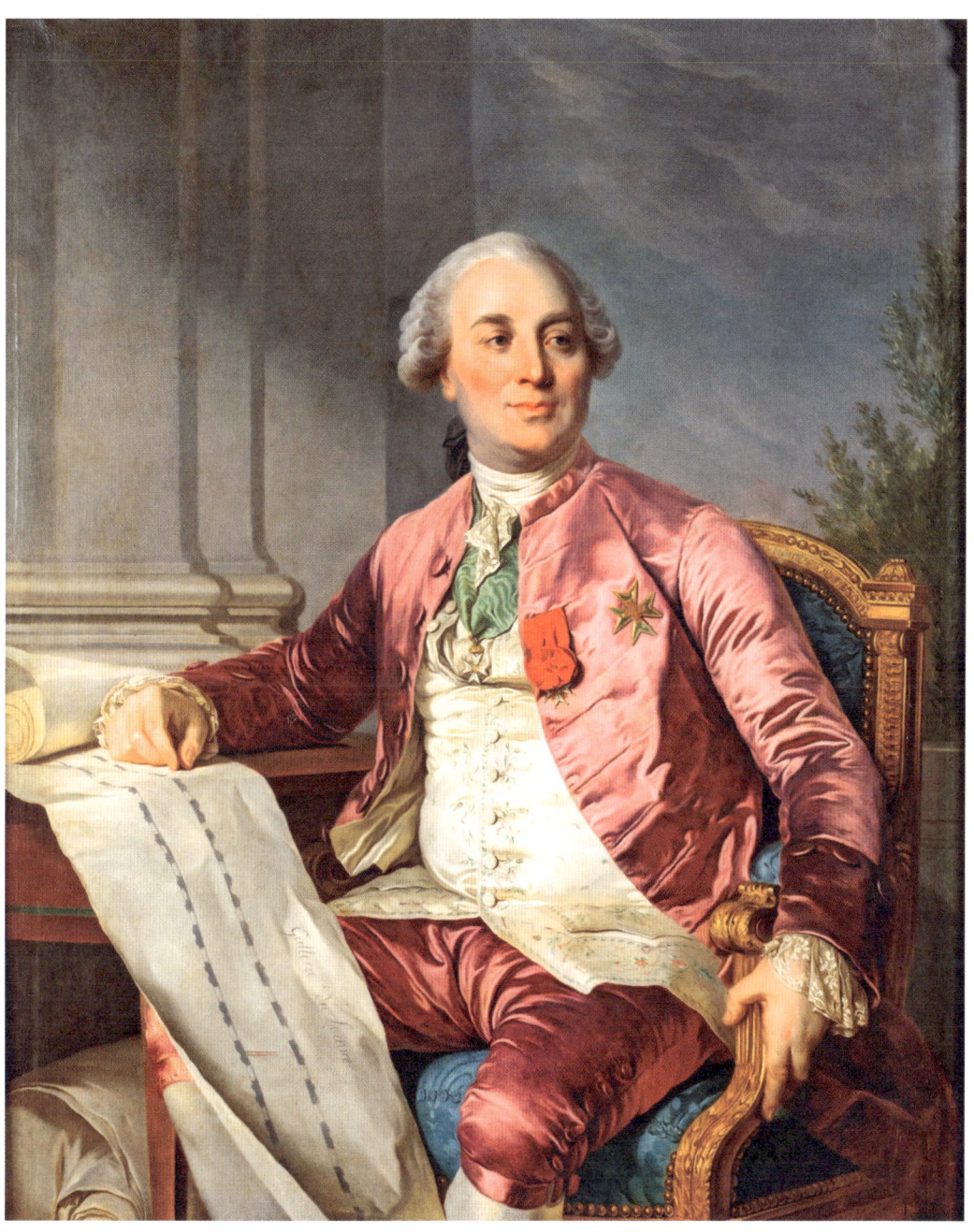

Le Domino Rose

1895

The Lady in Pink

La Belle Epoque consecrated the emergence of a carefree, festive elite in a society of harsh contrasts. In the United States, the ostentation of fashion spread amongst this newly established 'aristocracy'.

Americans adored fancy dress balls because they were often an opportunity to don historical European costumes, as if this legitimised their place in a world revering ancestral high society. The young woman portrayed here by John Humphreys Johnston is wearing an outfit particularly popular on such occasions. A domino is a silk, satin or cotton dress with ample sleeves and a hood, worn like a cape. Inspired by Venetian balls, it was often worn with a mask to complete the disguise.

Yet there is nothing festive about this picture. The model, seated in profile in front of an imposing piece of furniture, is looking away from us and down, seemingly lost in thought with a fan held absent-mindedly in her right hand. Has she slipped away from the ball for a moment of respite? Did she decide to have her portrait painted before making her entrance? Or was it merely the artist who chose to portray her like this?

John Humphreys Johnston had no need for additional adornments here. The domino, eclipsing its wearer, is the majestic, radiant star of the show. He is showing us the essence of high society, that appearances often count far more than the figures themselves. We must conform to social conventions in order to fit in. Is this young woman, wrapped in her domino, retiring for a few moments from a world uninterested in her true self?

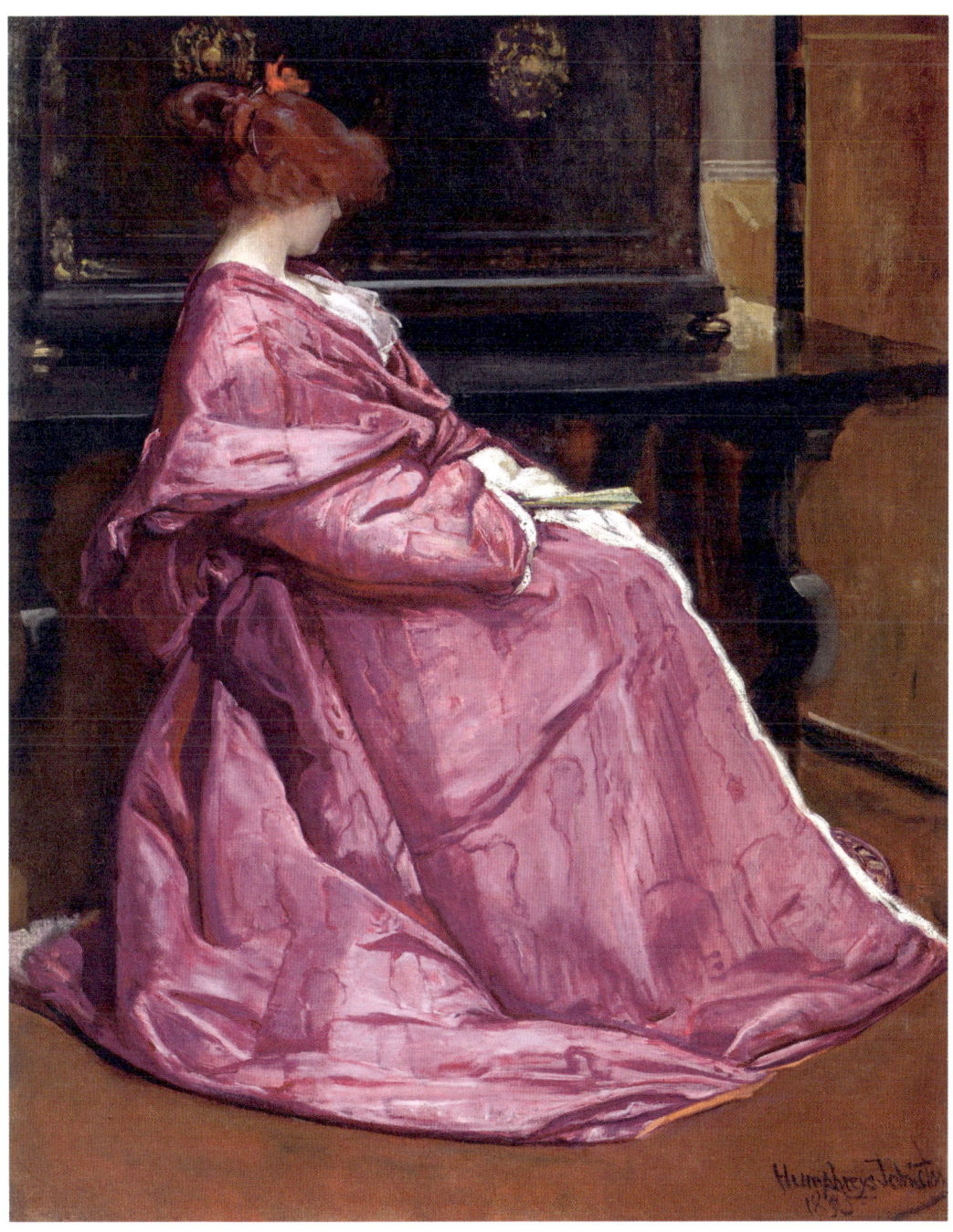

Le Domino Rose,
John Humphreys Johnston
1895
Oil on canvas
Museum of Fine Arts, Boston

Pot Pourri

1897

A Secret Woman

The Victorian painter Herbert James Draper specialised in mythological genre scenes flirting with the Pre-Raphaelite aesthetic. He also painted a number of pictures combining romanticism and realism.

Draper knew well that painting a woman with her back to us would prompt a host of interpretations. Who is this graceful, mysterious young woman gazing serenely downwards? Her radiant chestnut brown hair could almost be a halo. By dressing her in black Draper was accentuating the stark contrast between her figure and the rest of the composition.

We are separated from her by the roses and rose petals on the table. They add a poetic touch and we can almost smell their heady scent. With her delicate fingers she is preparing a *pot-pourri*, a meticulous, exquisite task but also a somewhat ambivalent one because roses have thorns.

And so we begin to see her in a different light. We realise that this woman has all the attributes of the fin-de-siècle femme fatale: the red hair, translucent complexion and black dress. Perhaps, like the rose, she too is full of contradictions: both gentle and sharp. She is engaged in a respectable, stereotypical female activity but she is also signifying that she cannot be reduced to that. In her mysterious presence we sense a world of secrets and desires.

Smelling of Roses

In Victorian times women were fond of perfuming themselves with eau de Cologne and also with flower essences, Perfume was not applied directly to the skin but on gloves, handkerchiefs or garments. Perfumed lip balms were also popular.

The Language of Flowers

Hyacinth: kindness
Rose: love
Rosemary: memory
Tulip: passion
Daffodil: reciprocal desire for love
Lavender: distrust
Basil: hate

It was the moon that had made her so pale, and there was something from the gods that enveloped her like a subtle vapour.

Gustave Flaubert

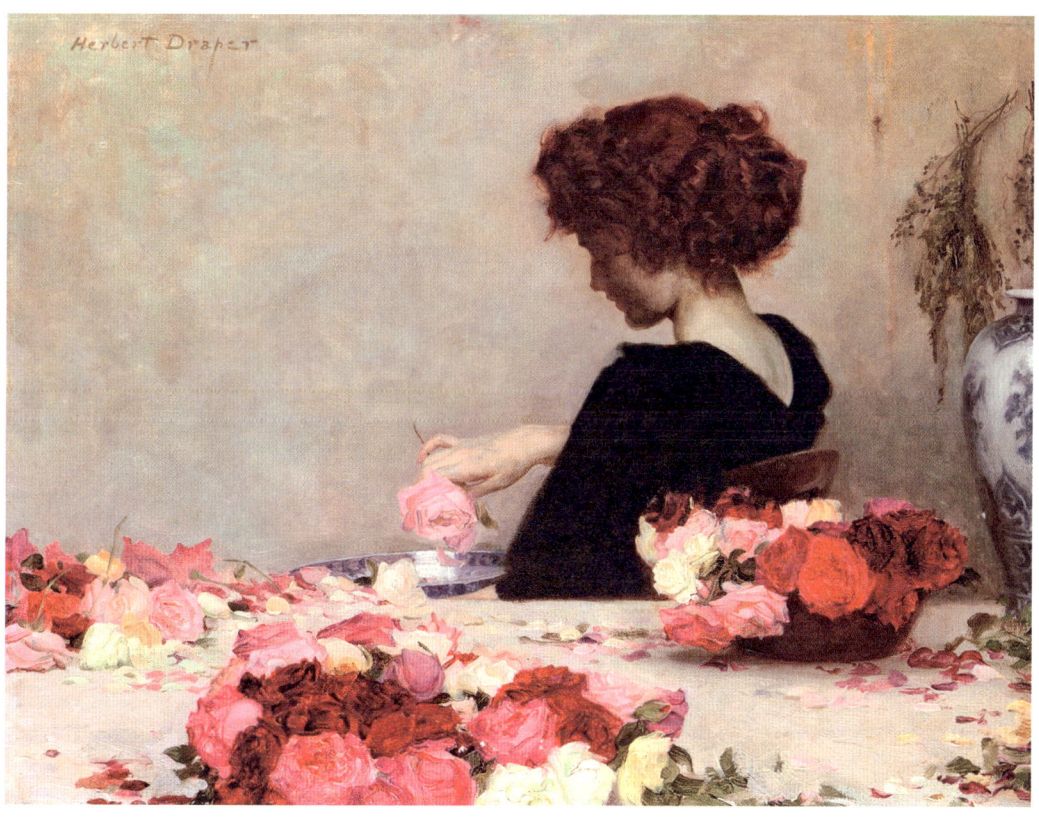

Pot Pourri,
Herbert James Draper
1897
Oil on canvas
Tate, London

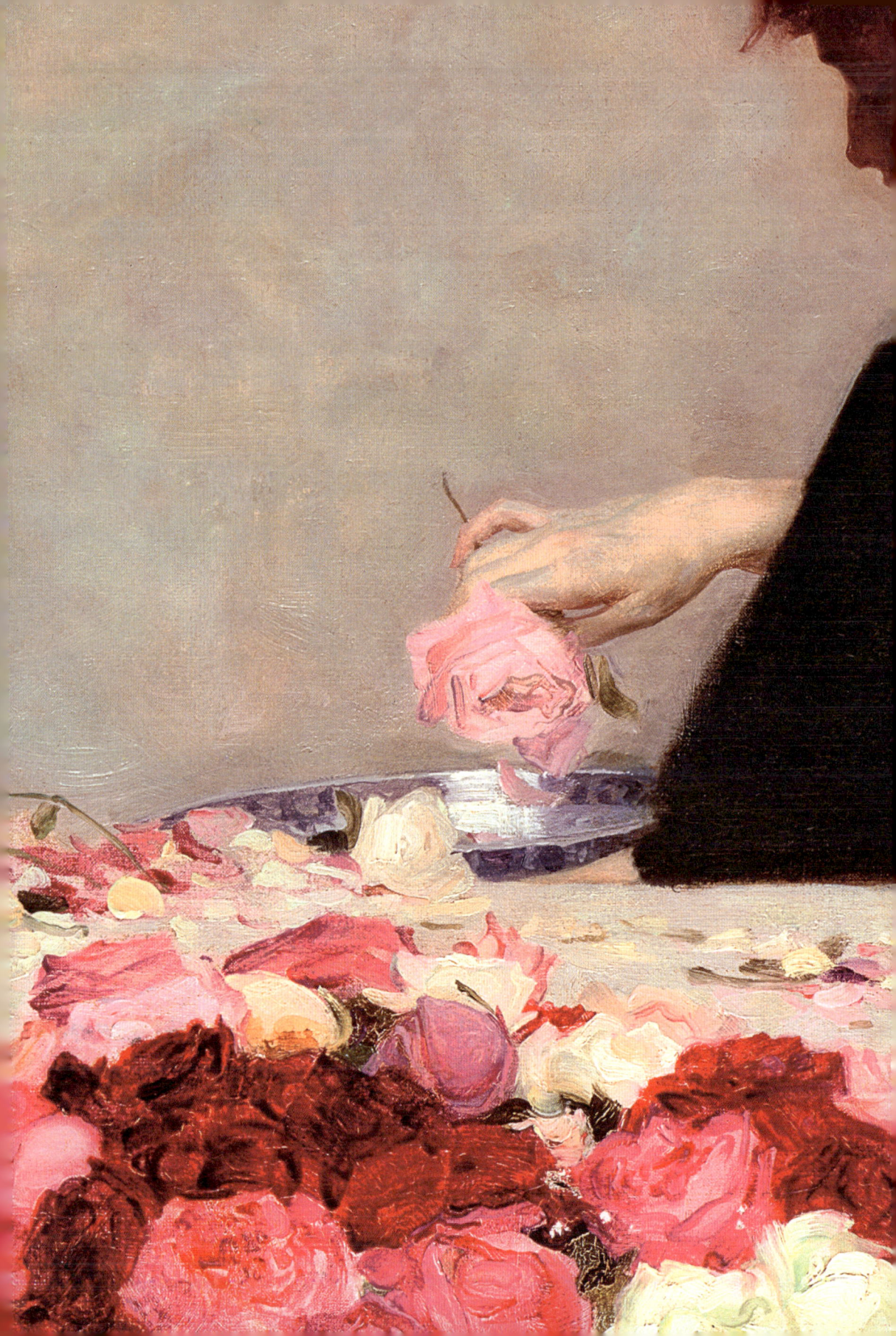

Six Dancers

1911

In Rhythm

Ernst Ludwig Kirchner played an active role in the group Die Brücke from 1905 and in the Expressionist movement that developed in Germany. He made colour a powerful narrative and psychological element in his work.

Dance was one of Kirchner's recurrent subjects, perhaps because he could express the vivacity of the body in movement and also because it allowed him to give free rein to his artistic sensitivity. The German Expressionists favoured tormented forms and vivid colours in a raw affirmation of creation and in his vibrant, nervous works Kirchner embraced this aesthetic.

In this lively composition, the dancers occupy almost all the picture space, both with their figures and the colour pink unifying their bodies and costumes, their pink tutus symbolising the world of classical dance.

As he often did, in this depiction of rhythmic movement Kirchner skillfully combined order and disorder. He emphasised movement with the bold outlines of the figures and angular lines of their arms and feet. Yet in doing so he also made the dancers' poses surprisingly rigid and strangely inanimate, like dolls. We sense his will to create a vibrant whole conveying the harmony of the choreography and music rather than dwelling on details. There are clear references to works by Cézanne, Van Gogh and Matisse. Emotion and expression were his prime concerns.

Skin Effects

The tutu appeared with Romanticism in the 1830s, shortly after the white or pink dance costume, in silk for the principal dancer, in cotton for the corps de ballet. Pink, close to flesh colour and heightening a mythical femininity, gives the dancers a sensual, erotic allure because they can appear to be almost nude.

Art Reviled

On 19 July 1937, the *Entartete Kunst* (Degenerate Art) exhibition opened in Munich. It comprised some seven hundred works removed from German museums, chosen by the Nazi authorities to epitomise their 'insult to German feeling'. These 'degenerate' works were then destroyed or sold. Kirchner, a victim of this censorship, committed suicide in 1938.

Dance, dance, otherwise we are lost.

Pina Baush

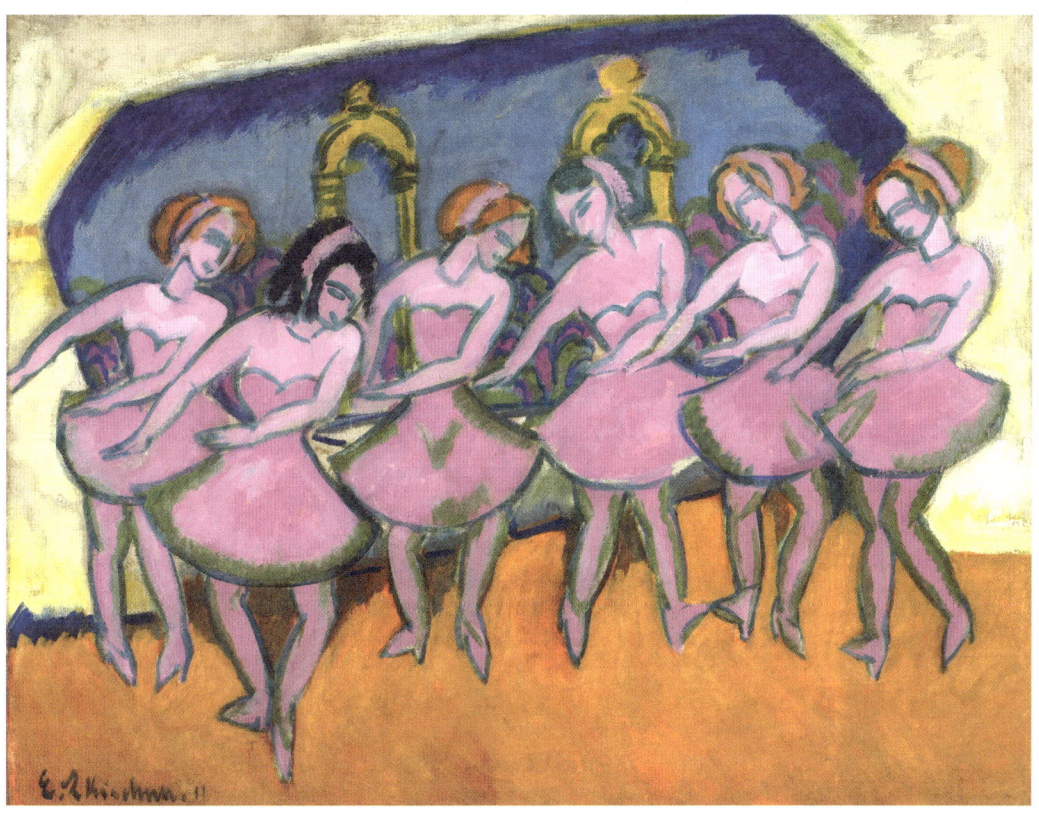

Six Dancers,
Ernst Ludwig Kirchner
1911
Oil on canvas
Virginia Museum of Fine Arts,
Richmond

Portrait of Baroness Gourgaud in a Pink Cape

1923

Woman, Women

At the beginning of her career Marie Laurencin frequented the Parisian avant-garde circles of the Fauves and Cubists. But in the 1910s she freed herself from these influences, developing a more personal style she called 'nymphism', whose dominant colours are pale grey, pink and pastel blue

In the Roaring Twenties she became the foremost portraitist of French high society and the aristocracy, excelling in vaporous portrayals of elegant, slender women which she liked to associate with animals to give them a fanciful, allegorical air.

Often described as mawkish by her detractors, Marie Laurencin painted a female ideal celebrating timeless grace and, for once, not subjected to male objectification.

This portrait of Baroness Gourgaud is a prime example of this. Although an oil painting, its pale, diluted tones could almost have been painted in watercolour. Her light pink garment and luminous pearls contrast with the almost monochrome grey backdrop. The dog on her lap seems rather unreal, as if placed there as an afterthought.

All of Marie Laurencin's portraits are similar yet different: always the same woman but never quite the same. One wonders whether the artist was exploring her own identity in them, in a society and an art world dominated by men negating her individuality.

Portrait of Baroness Gourgaud in a Pink Cape,
Marie Laurencin
1923
Oil on canvas
Centre Pompidou, musée national d'Art moderne, Paris

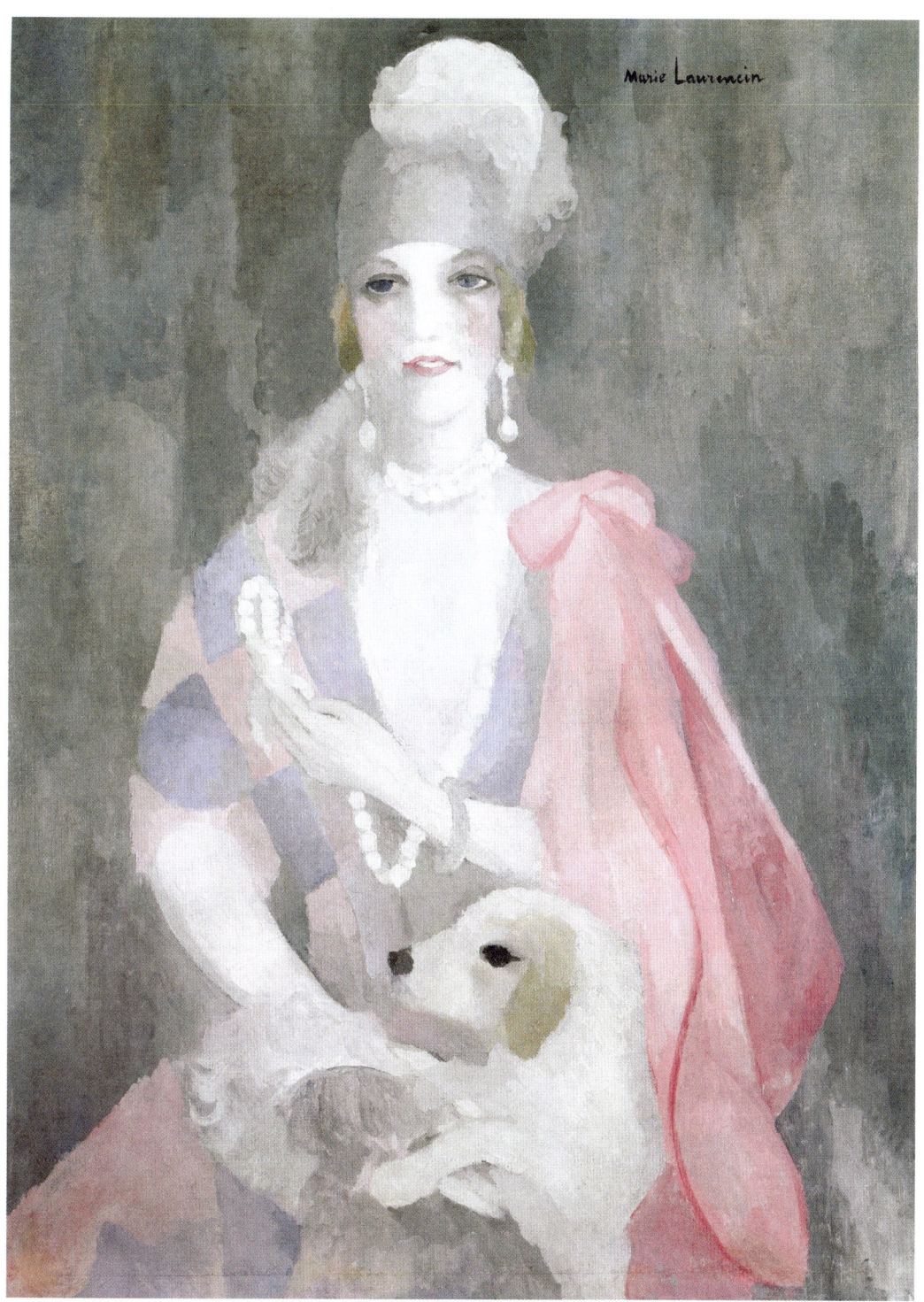

From Pink Shell

1931

TIMELINE

Seashells in Art

1483–1485	Sandro Botticelli, *The Birth of Venus*
	Giuseppe Arcimboldo, *Water* **1566**
1660	Pieter Boel, *Still Life with Fish*
	Alexandre Leroy de Barde, *Selection of Shells Arranged on Shelves* **1803**
1896	James Ensor, *Seashells*
	Le Corbusier, *Bather, Boat and Shell* **1938**
1941	Henri Matisse, *Still Life with a Magnolia*

An Elusive Secret

Georgia O'Keeffe emerged in the 1910s as one of the pioneers of American abstract art. Most of her contemporaries looked to industry for inspiration but she preferred observing the natural world.

Georgia O'Keeffe collected all kinds of things she found while out walking: flowers, bones, leaves, shells, etc. Once she had removed them from their environment, she gave them a new existence free of all references, concentrating solely on their rhythms, forms and colours. She often said that she had been fascinated by seashells since childhood, when she lived far from the ocean yet could touch it and listen to it when she held these wonderful creations to her ear.

In 1926 she produced her first series of shell paintings, neither figurative nor abstract, modulating their variations to explore her emotions. The fluctuating nuances of colour evoke a pink shell that we imagine rather than ever really seeing. Would we have recognised it as a shell without the title? This matters little, because what counted for Georgia O'Keeffe was plunging us into the depths of her soul, showing us what she felt when she gazed at this pink shell.

Much has been written on how Georgia O'Keeffe's works can evoke female intimacy, and this is certainly the case here. In this gentle, voluptuous, manifestly erotic painting, her arabesques of colour seem to be drawing us into the secrets of the female sex. A secret never revealed.

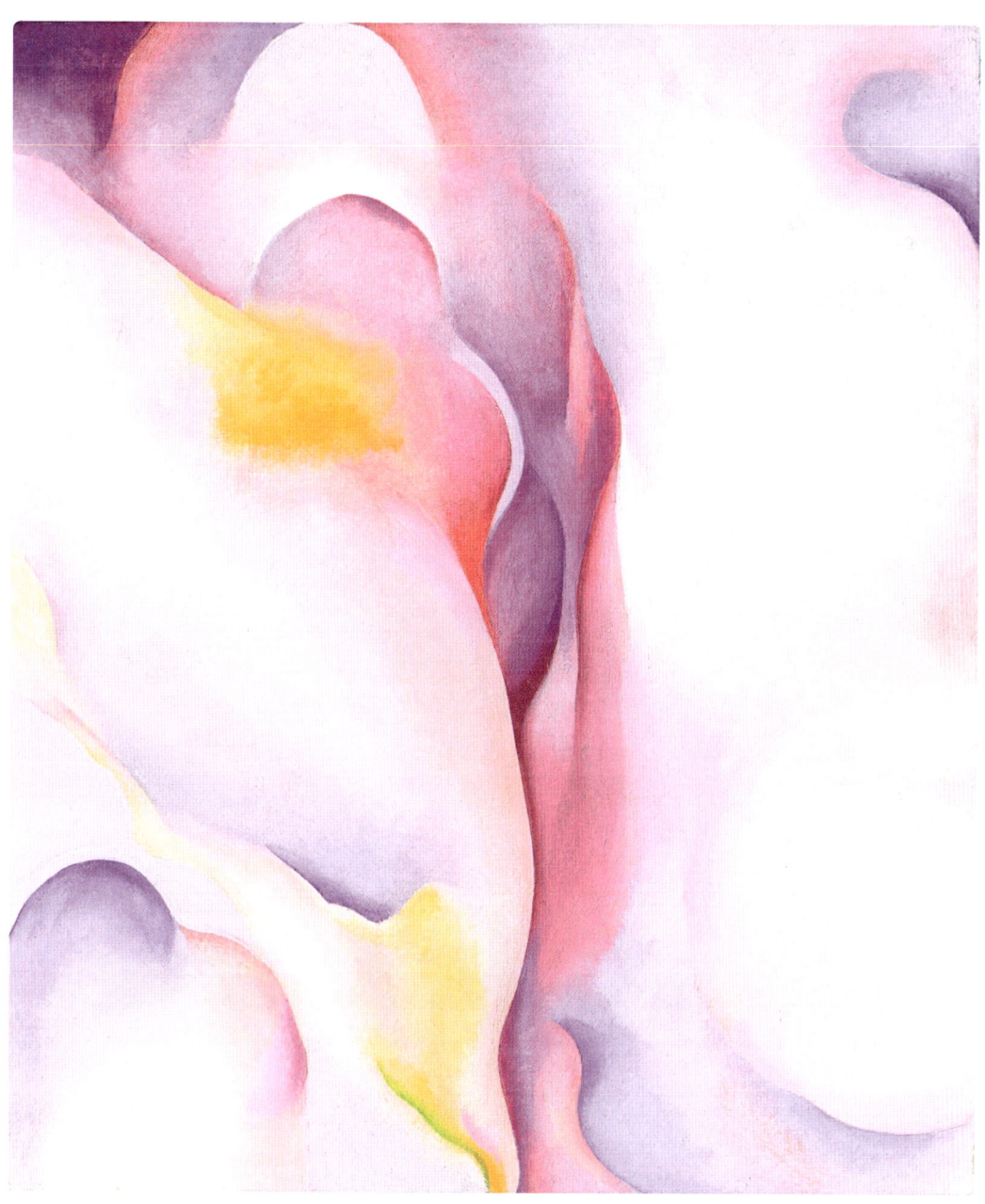

From Pink Shell,
Georgia O'Keeffe
1931
Oil on canvas
Private collection

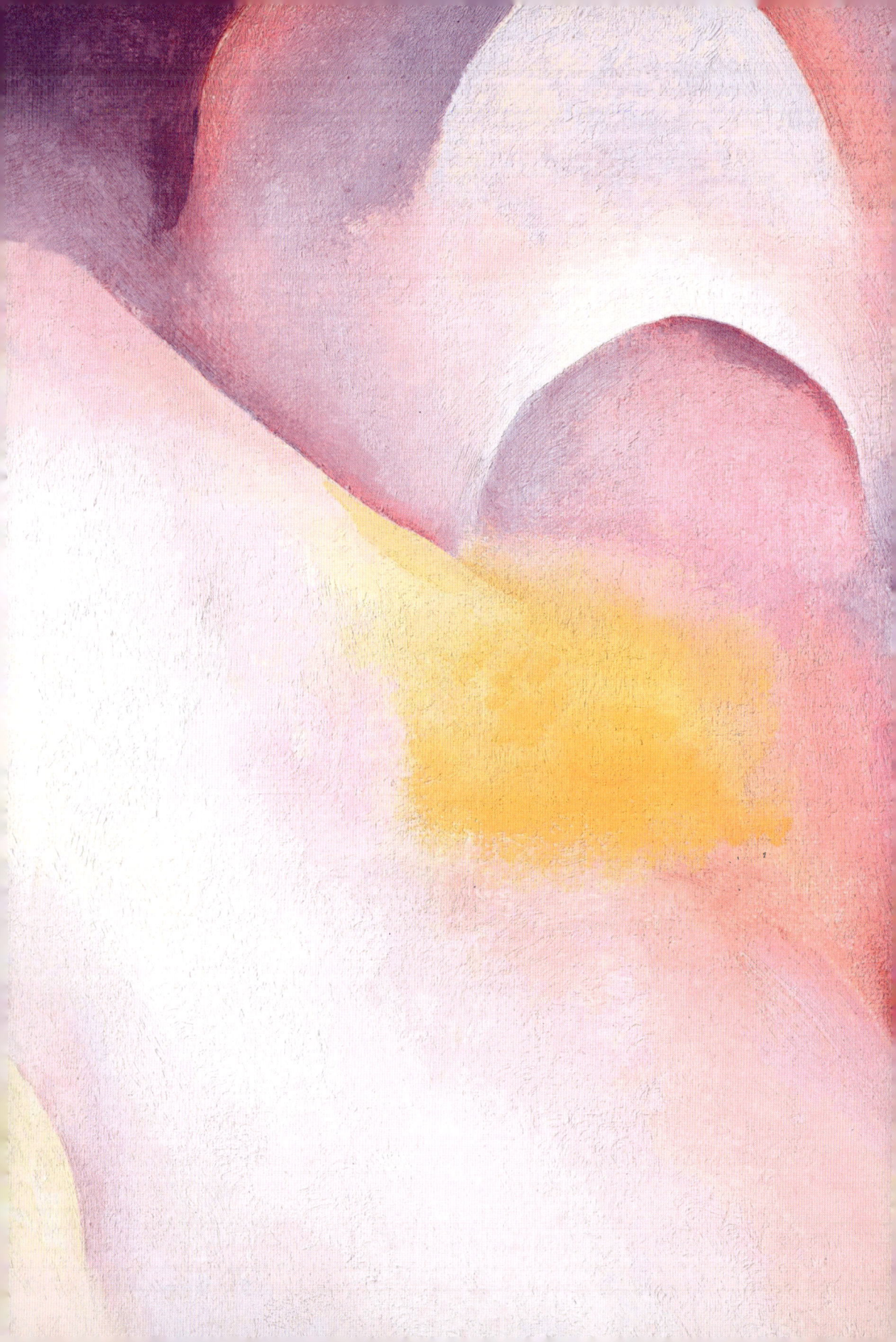

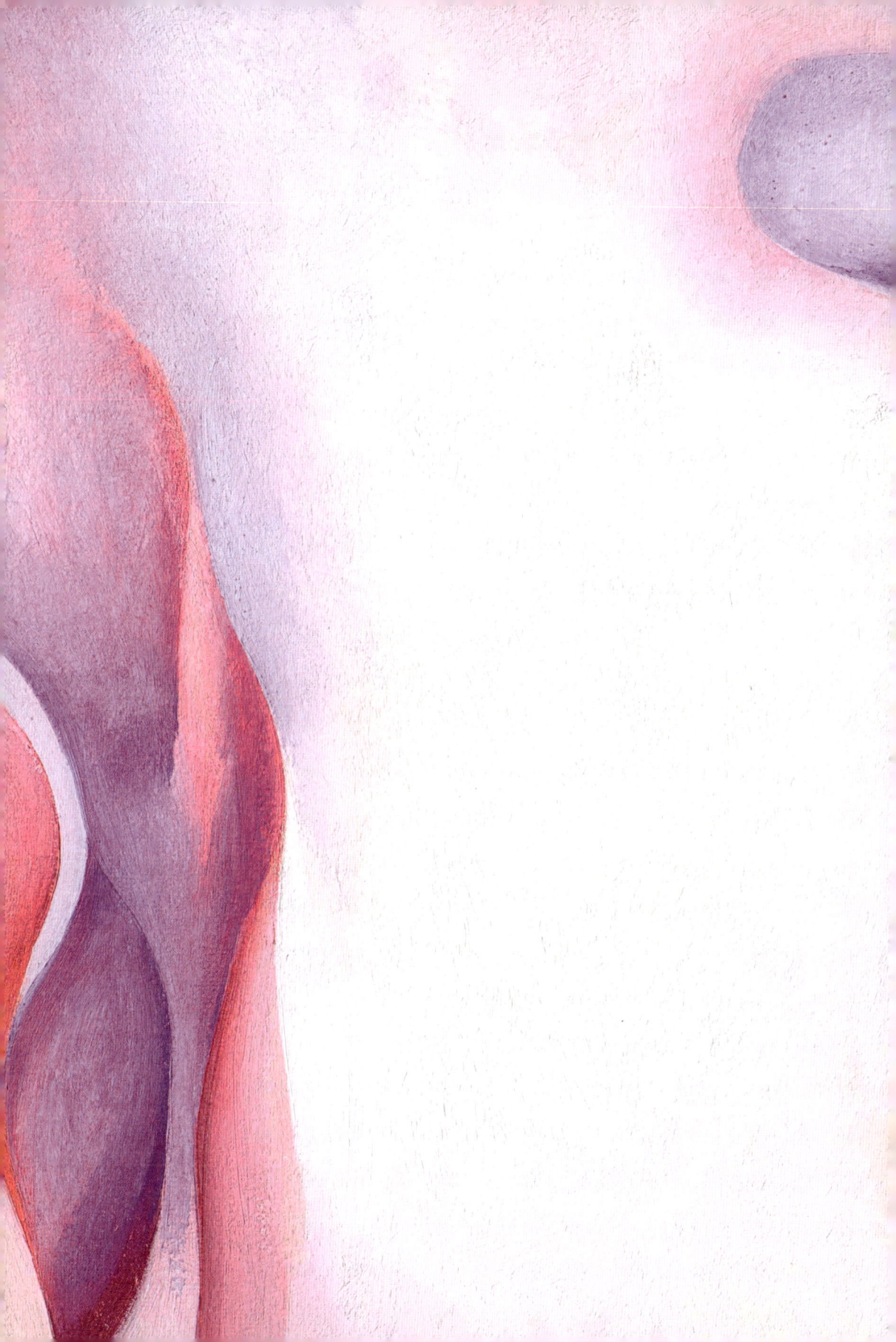

Self-Portrait on the Borderline Between Mexico and the United States

1932

TIMELINE
Fetish Pink

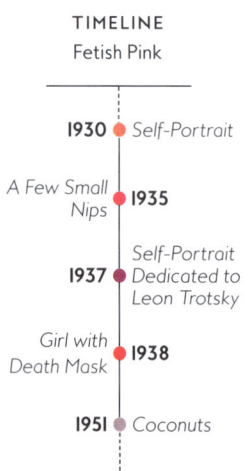

1930 • *Self-Portrait*

A Few Small Nips • 1935

1937 • *Self-Portrait Dedicated to Leon Trotsky*

Girl with Death Mask • 1938

1951 • *Coconuts*

I have two loves . . .

Frida Kahlo's work directly reflects her life, her questionings and her assertion of her identity as a female, Mexican artist. In 1932 she was living in the United States, having accompanied her husband, Diego Rivera, and this prompted her to contrast her origins with such a foreign, modern land.

Standing impassively like a statue on a possibly booby-trapped plinth on the Mexican-American border, Frida Kahlo is making it clear from the start. She is dividing the composition in two. On the left, symbols of ancient Mexico's Aztec architectural and artistic heritage and the country's luxuriant vegetation; on the right, the brave new world of industrialisation with its skyscrapers, machines and a polluting Ford factory (the couple were then living in Detroit).

Here Frida Kahlo is showing a certain nostalgia for a spiritual and ancestral Mexico guided by deified stars. Yet she has little faith in this because she depicts a decayed homeland in disarray with no longer any foundations. Just as her relationship with Mexico appears more ambivalent than one might think, her vision of the United States is not entirely devoid of admiration. She appreciates the modernity of the American way of life, portraying herself in an American-style pink dress contrasting with her love of traditional Mexican attire. She has a Mexican flag in her left hand and a cigarette, synonymous with freedom, in her right hand – in Mexico women were not permitted to smoke in public.

Standing steadfastly as an example, she is also showing us the roots of Mexican plants and industrial machinery mingling, inviting us to associate modernity and tradition.

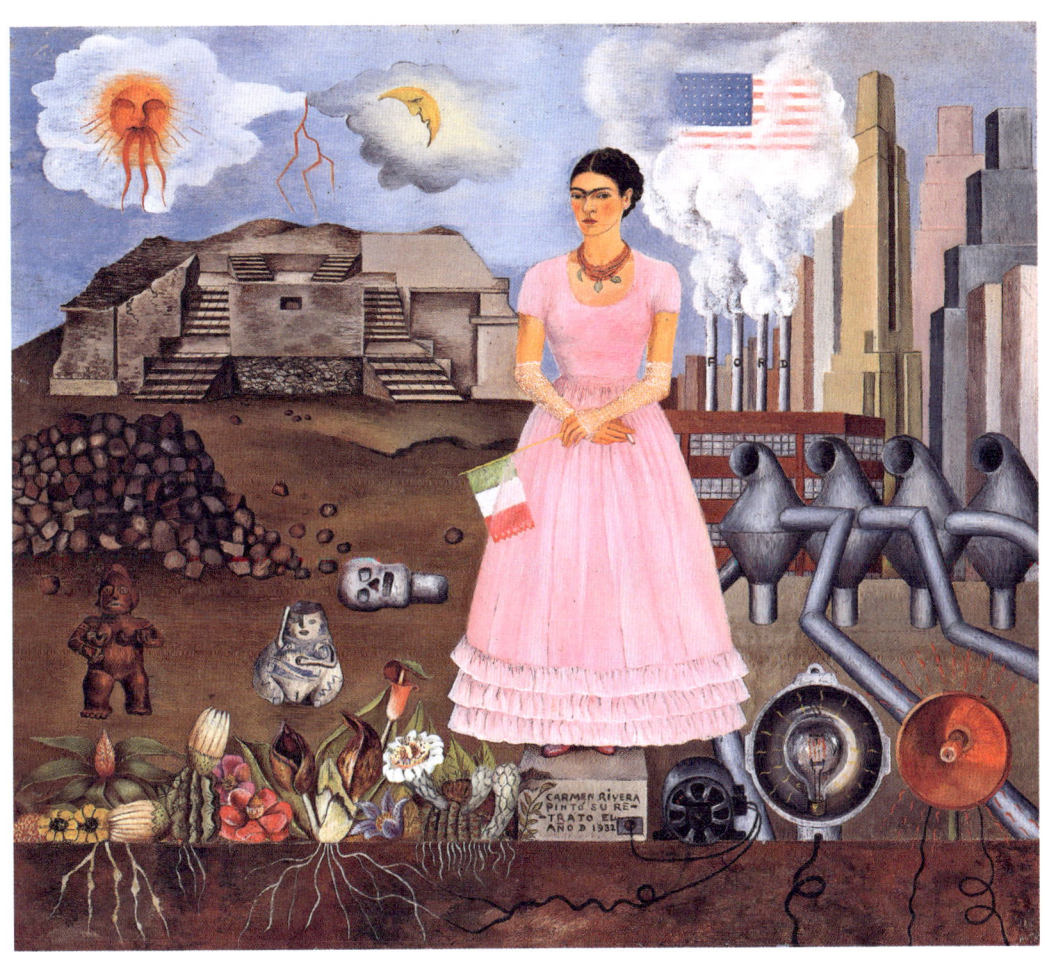

*Self-Portrait on the Borderline
Between Mexico and the United
States,*
Frida Kahlo
1932
Oil on metal
Private collection

Bâtons, La Rose, Impressions

1933

An Important Pink

In the 1910s Wassily Kandinsky gravitated increasingly towards abstraction, identifying his compositions with music to free them from figurative connotations. His combinations of geometric forms and colours were his pictures' sole source of narration.

In 1922 Kandinsky began teaching mural painting, form and analytical painting at the Bauhaus in Weimar. When the school was forced to close by the Nazis in 1933 he painted this rose, a very particular rose difficult to discern.

And is it really a rose? Or is it just shades of pink? Both? Kandinsky is inviting us to imagine what line or curve could evoke a flower. As was his habit, he played on colour harmonies, here the complementary and opposing blue and pink. Should we regard this as a male-female opposition: boys in blue, girls in pink?

Our eyes wander among the forms he scattered over the canvas, jumping from one to the other to some dynamic, musical rhythm. Caught in this movement, we begin to regard the picture as a kind of musical score whose staves, like crutches, are providing us with well needed support in this rather precarious disequilibrium. Kandinsky lost his job at the Bauhaus and had to leave Nazi Germany for Paris as a refugee. Did he depict a rose, incarnation of beauty, to forget the ugliness of the world?

Girl or Boy?

Until the 1930s babies and infants were usually dressed in easily washable white. Later, girls and boys began to be differentiated, initially with accessories then by increasingly identifying pink with girls and blue with boys, whereas historically it had been the opposite. Postwar fashion accentuated this tendency with the exaltation of femininity popularised by Christian Dior.

Fraud?

Controversy still endures as to who created the first abstract painting. Kandinsky or Hilma af Klint? Certain art historians have suspected that Kandinsky backdated one of his watercolours, dating it 1910 instead of 1913 . . .

It is thus evident that colour harmony can rest only on the principle of thecorresponding vibration of the human soul. This basis can be considered the principle of innermost necessity.

Wassily Kandinsky

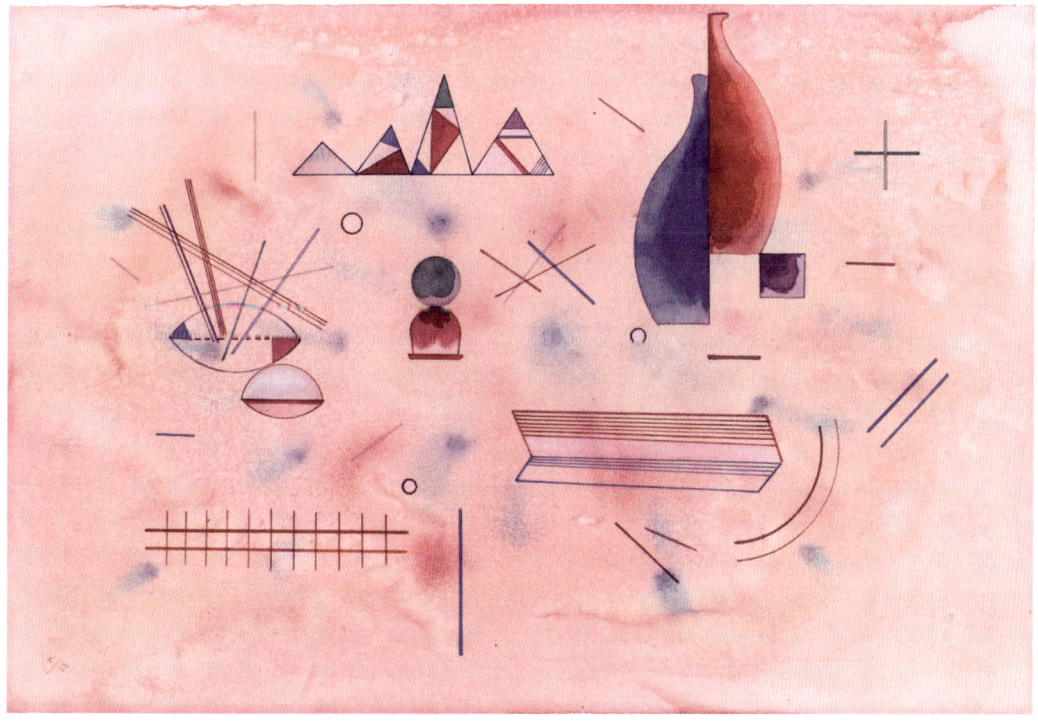

Bâtons, La Rose, impressions,
Wassily Kandinsky
1933
Watercolour, ink and gouache on
paper
Centre Pompidou, musée national
d'Art moderne, Paris

Polaroid Diary, 11.02.1993, Madrid

1993

A Pink for Everyone

In 2016 Pantone devised a pink, dubbed 'Millennial pink' and elected 'Colour of the Year' when on social media it came to epitomise the global conversation on gender identity. Many described it as a 'non-colour', but it is definitely a pink that transcends gender stereotypes because it was adopted by both men and diehard feminists.

Feminine/ Masculine

According to Eva, to recognise the other sex in oneself is the beginning of an understanding, the beginning of a solution to female-male antagonism.

A Life, a Work

The *Polaroid Diary* series consists of some 1,500 self-portraits taken daily with a Polaroid camera by the artists EVA & ADELE before they went out. It illustrates their intent to negate the barrier between public and private life.

EVA & ADELE regard their lives and relationship as an artistic creation in itself. They have never revealed their real names or origins and have invented a story for themselves beginning when they met in 1989, when they returned from the future to question the notion of gender.

With their shaved heads, excentric makeup and carefully chosen outfits, they could be hermaphrodites or even Siamese twins, representing themselves in this way to create a kind of constant 'happening' wherever they go. EVA & ADELE exist as much in the supermarket as they do at the major art fairs. Their appearances are performances and their performance is their life.

The couple have been redefining gender differences since Eva, male at birth, decided to modify her gender to marry Adele. Nevertheless, they do not regard themselves as women, preferring the idea that they have invented their own, new gender and celebrating this fusion as a sign of unconditional love. EVA & ADELE chose this transgression to more fully demonstrate how blurred sexual identity can be, showing themselves in a candy pink loaded with female connotations, yet shaving their heads like men and exaggerating stereotypes to better reveal their falsehood.

Polaroid Diary, 11.02.1993,
Madrid,
EVA & ADELE
1993
Polaroid photograph
Galerie Nicole Gnesa, Munich

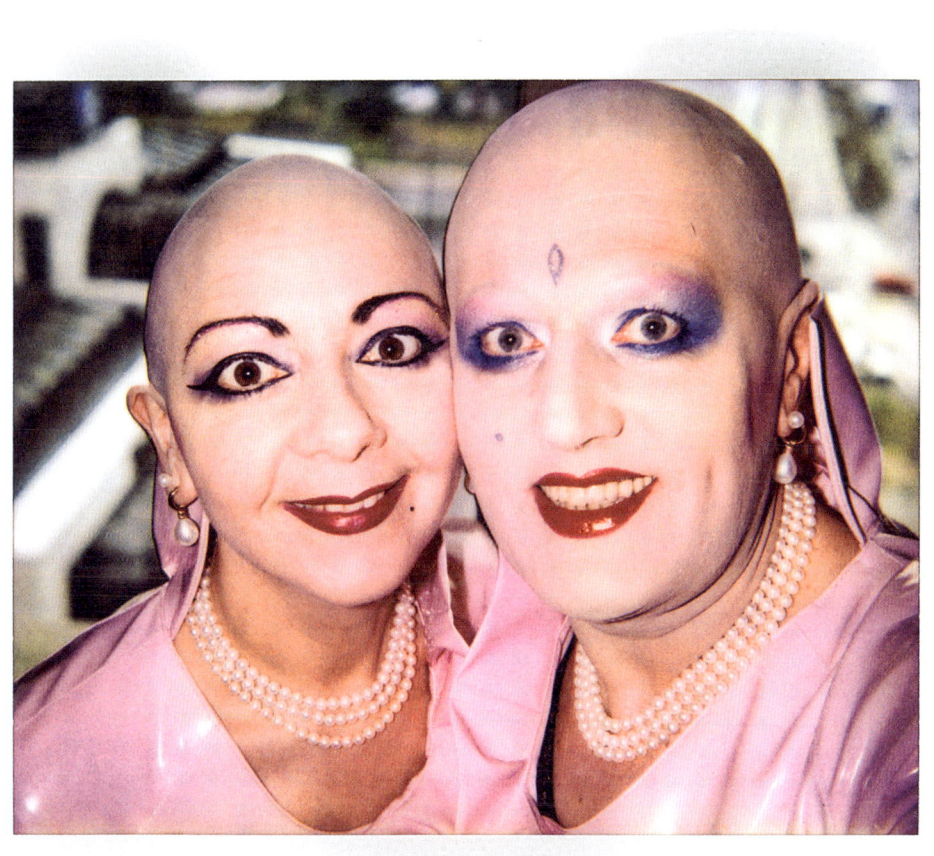

Wherever we are is museum.

EVA & ADELE

Just Love Me

1998

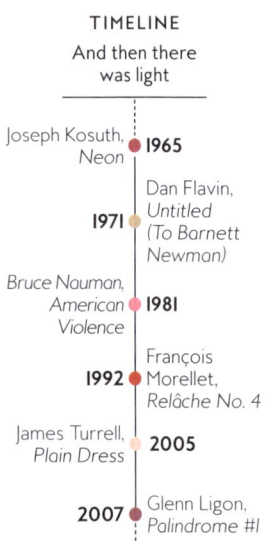

TIMELINE
And then there
was light

Joseph Kosuth,
Neon — **1965**

1971 — Dan Flavin,
Untitled
(To Barnett
Newman)

Bruce Nauman,
American — **1981**
Violence

1992 — François
Morellet,
Relâche No. 4

James Turrell,
Plain Dress — **2005**

2007 — Glenn Ligon,
Palindrome #1

Love or Nothing

In the 1980s and 90s the Young British Artists embodied a new generation that revolutionised the creative process and also their own media exposure via their controversial, wild lifestyles.

Tracey Emin was one of the artists discovered by the collector Charles Saatchi. A hallmark of her work is her completely uncensored sharing of her private life, which she explores in various forms, ranging from installations to drawings, paintings and neon creations.

In her neon works, words and phrases are written in an often fluorescent pink cursive scrawl crudely expressing the full range of her emotions, hopes and experiences. For Tracey Emin, there can be no pretence: the ugly, sad and ridiculous all have their role to play. Her life is her work. She is her sole, exhibitionistic and yes, narcissistic subject.

So, to whom is this plea – 'Just Love Me' – addressed? To us? Is Tracey Emin asking for our forgiveness, tolerance, mercy? She seems to be asking us to love her despite everything, despite our annoyance and irritation. Is she seeking some kind of approval or is she merely sharing a sentiment? Who is she asking for affection from?

As is often the case, the personal is also collective, because 'Just Love Me' is something we all hope for. Many are the situations in which this appeal returns. By turning the neon light on herself, Tracey Emin is illuminating what links or separates us from others: the universal longing to be loved.

Just Love Me,
Tracey Emin
1998
Neon tube
Private collection

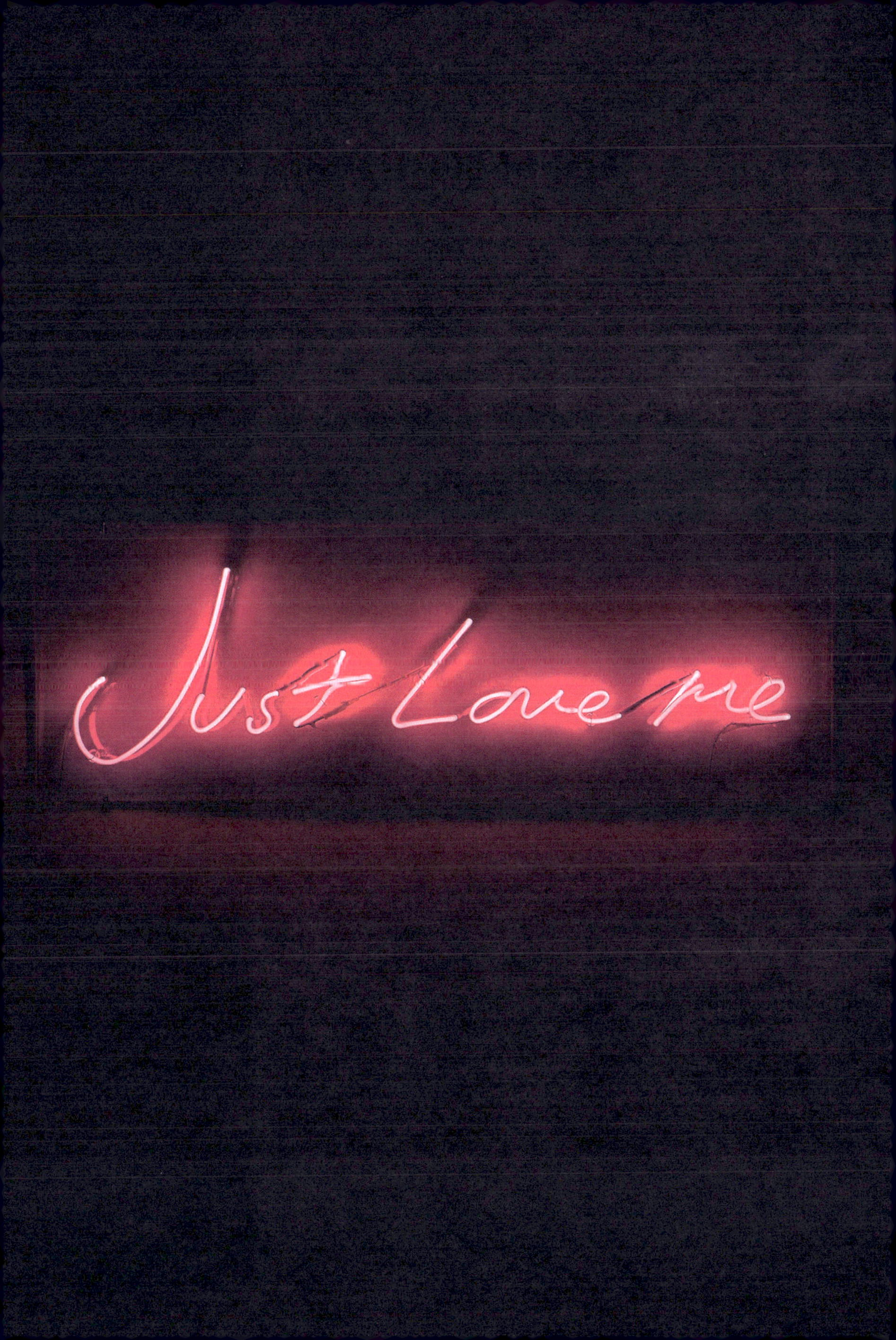
Just Love me

List of Illustrations

Photographic credits

© Adagp, Paris, 2021 / Photo RMN Grand Palais / Bulloz: 51, 52–53
© Archives Alinari, Florence, Dist. RMN-Grand Palais / Raffaello Bencini: 19, 20–21
© Alamy / Artiz: 5, 85 / Peter Barritt: 49
© Banco de México Diego Rivera Frida Kahlo Museums, 2021 / Adagp, Paris / Photo Bridgeman: 4, 99
© Bridgeman Images: 9, 16, 35, 39 / Fine Art Images: 75 / Graphica Artis: 3, 31 / Luisa Ricciarini: 25 / Royal Collection Trust, Her Majesty Queen Elizabeth II, 2021: 73 / The Maas Gallery, London: 87, 88–89
© CC0 Public Domain: Accademia Nazionale di San Luca: 69, 70–71 / Kunsthistorisches Museum Wien: 63 / Metropolitan Museum of Art New York: 65 (49.7.5, The Jules Bache Collection), 77 (55.121.10.24, Rogers Fund and The Kevorkian Foundation Gift) / Nelson-Atkins Museum of Art, William Rockhill Nelson Trust: 27, 28–29 / Paris Musées, Petit Palais (PPP439): 37 / Pérez Simón Collection, Mexico: 14–15, 41 / Virginia Museum of Fine Arts: 60–61, 91 (2009.171, Ludwig and Rosy Fischer Collection, Bequest of Anne R. Fischer), 79 (37.2631, Walters Art Museum, Baltimore)
© Centre Pompidou, MNAM-CCI, Dist. RMN-Grand Palais / Philippe Migeat: 101
© Château de Versailles, Dist. RMN-Grand Palais / Christophe Fouin: 81, 83
© Courtesy of the parish of San Michele Arcangelo, Carmignano: 67
© Estate of Christo V. Javacheff / Adagp, Paris, 2021 / Photo Wolfgang Volz: 55
© Fondation Foujita / Adagp, Paris, 2021: 93
© Georgia O'Keeffe / Adagp, Paris, 2021 / Photo Christie's: 2, 95, 96–97
© RMN-Grand Palais / Château de Pau, Didier Sorbé: 23 / Musée d'Orsay, Hervé Lewandowski: 43, 44–45
© Succession Picasso 2021 / Photo Bridgeman Images: 47
© Takashi Murakami / Photo Christie's: 59
© The Easton Foundation / Adagp, Paris 2021 / Photo The Museum of Modern Art, New York / Scala, Florence: 57Request for help
© The Wallace Collection, Dist. RMN-Grand Palais / The Trustees of the Wallace Collection: 33
© Tracey Emin. All rights reserved / Adagp, Paris, 2021 / Photo Phillips Auction: 105
© EVA & ADELE / VG Bildkunst, Bonn / Adagp, Paris, 2021 / courtesy: Nicole Gnesa Galerie, Munich: 103

Impressum

First published in French by
© Hachette Livre (Éditions du Chêne), 2021
Original title: Rose. De Botticelli à Christo

© Prestel Verlag, Munich · London · New York 2026
A member of Penguin Random House Verlagsgruppe GmbH
Neumarkter Strasse 28 · 81673 Munich

1st edition 2026

produktsicherheit@penguin-randomhouse.de
(The above information is mandatory information according to GPSR and should be used for all queries relating to the safety of our books)

The publisher expressly reserves the right to exploit the copyrighted content of this work for the purposes of text and data mining in accordance with Section 44b of the German Copyright Act (UrhG), based on the European Digital Single Market Directive. Any unauthorized use is an infringement of copyright and is hereby prohibited.

A CIP catalogue record for this book is available from the British Library.
Library of Congress Control Number: 2025946693

Éditions du Chêne:
Director: Emmanuel Le Vallois
Edition: Hélène Sevin
Art director: Sabine Houplain
Graphic design: Sophie Della Corte assisted by Audrey Alves
French proofreaders: Clémentine Bougrat, Clothilde Bollard Duval
Production: Rémy Chauvière
Separations: Reproscan

Translation: David Wharry
Copyediting: Russell Stockman
Editorial direction Prestel: Markus Eisen
Production management: Martina Effaga
Typesetting: Uhl+Massopust GmbH
Printing and binding: M Paper, Huizhou, China

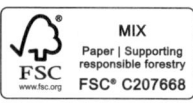

Penguin Random House Verlagsgruppe FSC® N001967

Printed in China

ISBN 978-3-7913-9430-5

www.prestel.com